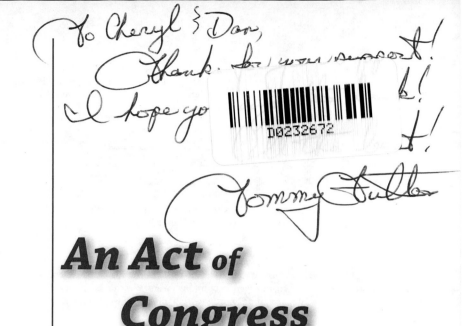

To Cheryl & Dan,
Thank ... for your support.
I hope yo ...
...
Tommy Fulton

An Act of

Congress

The Real-Life Story of
Power and Politics
in Family Business

Tommy Fulton

Lucid Style
Author Services

This work represents the author's recollection and interpretation of true events, based upon his own experiences, court documents, letters, audio recordings, and recollections from others who were involved.

THE FORUM FOR
FAMILY BUSINESS
ADDRESSING REAL-LIFE ISSUES OF COMMUNICATION
SUCCESSION AND PRESERVATION

Visit the author's Web site at www.TommyFulton.com
www.ForumForFamilyBusiness.com

Cover design and artwork by Eric J. Turman and Creative 2 a T, Inc.
Cover photo © Copyright 2008 JupiterImages
Back cover portrait of Tommy Fulton © Copyright 2007 M & A Studios
Aerial photograph of the Finch Companies, Inc. © 1993 Thigpen Photography
Newspaper articles courtesy of the Mobile Press Register, Mobile, Ala.,
reproduced with permission

Court documents are taken from *H. L. Callahan v. Thomas W. Fulton, Elizabeth J. Fulton, Daniel R. Fulton, Samuel C. Fulton, The Finch Companies, an Alabama Corporation*, CV-91-001266, (Mobile County Circuit Court, Mobile, Ala., 1991); and *Thomas W. Fulton, Elizabeth J. Fulton, Daniel R. Fulton and Samuel C. Fulton v. H. L. Callahan*, Case No. 1910611 (Alabama Supreme Court, 1993)

Published by Lucid Style Author Services, 2008
Book design, layout, and editing by Jean A. Turman
Lucid Style Author Services
www.Creative2aT.com

ISBN: 978-0-9821992-0-6

Library of Congress Control Number: 2008939681

Printed in the USA

Table of Contents

to the extreme the political ambitions and financial desires of their minority co-owner, the true nature of his character became revealed only when they balked at his demands that they buy him out at his highly inflated price. He then initiated a heart-breaking lawsuit—one in which political clout had a devastating impact on the majority owners, out of which no winners emerged, and from which the loving ties that bind a family were forever severed.

In sharing his family's nightmarish experience with you, Tom Fulton has not only achieved a personal catharsis; their story emphatically confirms that EVERY family business needs thoughtful and realistic planning for succession.

I would also like to add this personal observation. I was and remain deeply touched by the Fultons' unyielding sense of honor and integrity throughout their troubled time. It permeated every aspect of their dealings with each other, with their employees, and with the world at large. Not once, not even in the darkest hours of their ordeal, did any of them ever falter from adhering to their ideals or from the certainty of knowing that in the end, they would get their company back. Indeed, they did.

Brock B. Gordon
Big Canoe, Georgia

September, 2008

Prologue

For years, as I told people the inside story of our family business succession battles, I heard time and again that I should write a book about it. I always said that I would do that someday. It has been more than a dozen years since the final determination of our experience. As I went through all of the documentation, including letters, financials, and especially all of the court documents, the rage and disbelief built up inside of me again. I saw many opportunities that both sides of our family could have taken which would have prevented the travesty that ensued. Maybe the families would have gone their separate ways, but perhaps we could have done it in a much more genial manner.

This story is my recollection, supported by thousands of pages of court documents, letters, audio recordings, and firsthand stories from those who were involved. This is a story of what happens when family businesses do not properly plan for the future. No matter how much one generation thinks, "things will fall into place at the proper time," unless you plan for smooth succession, disaster is probably waiting. I know…you should always backup your computer hard drive and have proper insurance. How many times do we have to wish we had prepared before we do the hard work required to avoid calamity?

When I was young, I vividly remember the joy and excitement of family get-togethers with the Fultons and Callahans. My parents had three kids, and my mother's cousin Sonny Callahan and his first wife Pat had four kids. After Pat's untimely death, Sonny remarried and had two more children.

All of us were close and enjoyed spending family time together. One of the challenges of family businesses, and the reason so many of these ventures fail in the third generation, is the neglect of a real plan of how everyone is going to fit in. The conclusion I've reached is that everyone rarely does fit in.

One of the people I asked to read the original draft of this book told me that I needed to decide why I was writing it. Did I want to use it as a "catharsis," or did I want to get revenge? Was this just a chance to retell my side of the story? The reason he asked me these things is because my first draft seemed more like two or three books to him. I appreciated his advice. (Interestingly, he thought I didn't sound quite mad enough about what had happened.)

The real reason I wrote this book is that I believe the best way to learn life's lessons is to learn from other people's errors. Any family succession expert can read this book and see at least a dozen moments when either side could have made more effective and intelligent decisions. I'm hoping that the reader will learn from our mistakes and work in a way that makes the "handing over of the baton" an exciting and fruitful experience for everyone involved.

When our families ended up in court, we found out later that there were several attorneys watching our case to see what precedent would be set. Some of these lawyers represented minority shareholders and some of them represented the majority. When all was said and done, the attorneys just shook their heads and told their clients that there was no precedent because the case had been handled in such a bizarre way. Maybe our case was not a good example for attorneys to use, but the story behind it gives lesson after lesson to business owners as well as estate and succession planners.

Acknowledgments

I suppose everyone goes through major challenges at various times throughout their lives. I found it very rewarding and humbling to discover who you can count on when those challenges get you down. We had numerous supporters who wished us well and promised to pray for us.

Many others were disgusted with what happened and wanted to lash out in some way. Those who kept us in their prayers are forever in our debt.

It's easy to be cynical when it comes to attorneys; after all, you pay them to be your advocate—not to believe in you. Our family is extremely grateful to Watson Smith, Brock Gordon, and Alan Christian for their dedication to our cause. They became members of our family and they let us know how much they did believe in us. They are a credit to their profession.

Steve Mixon took on the unenviable task of representing us on the Finch board of directors, knowing that he was badly outnumbered. Steve remains a close friend of our family to this day. Jim Cochran agreed to serve on that same board. Jim was a real-estate appraiser, and his help to us was a true sign of friendship. Billy Kimbrough also spent time on that board as our representative. Billy was an attorney with a reputation for toughness, which was invaluable to us in this outmanned situation.

What was most heartwarming to the Fulton family, though, were the people whose livelihood depended on decisions that our family made. With the exception of two or three of our more than one hundred employees, we will always be grateful for their support. In so many cases, it would have been easy for many of them to walk away. I believe to this day that they didn't because we tried so hard to make our "family" business inclusive of everyone who worked there. Several of these people put themselves at risk by making sure we were aware of everything that was happening at our company. To Bruce Byrd, Marcia Washam, Louise Cotton, Betsy Swinson, Kim Welch, Ed Alexander, Jeff Sims, and Mark Westbrook, your support will never be forgotten by any of the Fulton family.

Most of all, I know the pain and sacrifice my brother, Danny, and his wife, Angela, endured mostly as a result of decisions that I made. Not once did they seek to place the blame on me for all of the hell visited upon us. I was proud and grateful for their love and support…after all, he and I were thrown out of the company at the same time. Angela was in the very late stages of pregnancy and I can only imagine how tough it must have been on her.

I can't say enough about my wife, Lane, and her love and support during those times. With five children under the age of seven, she never wavered as we met the challenges. We've been married for more than twenty-seven years now, and I will forever be grateful beyond words for how she stood with me. The example she gave to our children will be a lesson they can use for the rest of their lives.

Our family benefited the most, however, from the love, support, and leadership of two of the most special people I've ever known in my life. My parents, S. C. and Betty Jo Fulton, did not deserve to go through any of this mess. Everyone involved marveled at their strength and durability. Mom died on December 15, 2003, and Dad died on August 25, 2006. Our memories of their dignity and class will stay with our family and friends for the rest of our lives. This book is dedicated to both of them.

Chapter One
The Finch Family Business

The Great Depression should have been the absolute worst time to start a new business venture. It seemed like an even worse time to challenge your boss when he tells you that you can either remain with your company at half pay or hit the road. My grandfather, Thomas William Finch, was in that exact situation in early 1933. He chose to hit the road.

He opened his new company, Finch Warehousing, on Mardi Gras Day in 1933, in downtown Mobile, Alabama. Tom Finch asked Kellogg Sales to leave his former employer and come on board as his first customer. They agreed, but only if it could be done quickly. It was done.

Downtown Mobile was everything a small port city would seem to be in the early thirties. The 10,000-square-foot building, a two-story warehouse, was located on Commerce Street just a couple of streets away from the Mobile River. My grandmother, Genevieve Fisher Finch, recounted those nerve-wracking days in a 1983 Mobile Press Register article. She said they leased the building for $50 a month, borrowed $300 against some stock, rented a truck, and spent Mardi Gras Day moving Corn Flakes. Soon after, they signed up two other accounts, Dole Pineapple and Diamond Matches (I can't even begin to imagine how in the world you could store something as volatile as matches under today's restrictive rules).

Even with the challenges all businesses had during this period, the company grew and added space to their downtown facilities. One of the employees suggested that they get into the moving business in addition to the commercial storage operations. They began as an agent for Delcher Van Lines. The moving business became a major focus of Finch Warehousing & Transfer and took a major jump in 1939, when the Finches became agents for Allied Van Lines, who promoted themselves over the years as "The World's Largest Movers."

In that Mobile Press Register article, Genevieve Finch described some of the challenges they encountered. One of my favorites is the story about what happened anytime there was a heavy rain. Downtown streets would flood, so they would move all of the items from the ground floor to the second floor, then sandbag the doors downstairs in an effort to keep out the water. The ceilings would sag threateningly, and they watched while huge rats negotiated the "rapids" on Commerce Street.

In 1956, the Finches realized a long-time dream...to build their own free-standing warehouse and home office complex, 56,000 square feet, on Telegraph Road. This location proved to be vital in later years, as the paper mills grew and thrived just a few miles away. The company operated on an even keel for the next eight years, until Tom Finch died in 1964.

Noteworthy changes during one's childhood sometimes come suddenly and without warning. In 1964, we were living in base housing on McDonnell Air Force Base, Wichita, Kansas. Just before the Little League baseball season was to begin for me, I remember lying in bed, thinking about playing ball and a new bicycle I was going to have. I heard the phone ring. Moments later, I heard my mother crying on the phone and asking my father, "What are we going to do…what are we going to do?" My grandfather, Thomas William Finch, had died in Mobile, Alabama, of a sudden, unanticipated heart attack.

Life was about to change quickly. We woke up early the next morning, packed a few things, and left for Mobile. It's funny, the things you remember the rest of your life. My best friend, Joe Hannigan, lived across the street from us. Before we left, I went over to his house, knocked on the door, and faced his mother in the doorway. "Can I see Joe for a minute?" I asked. She told me he had to finish his breakfast first. I never had the chance to see him again.

From that point on, I would live all of my non-college years in Mobile, Alabama. My Dad received a hardship transfer to Mobile as an air traffic controller for the U.S. Air Force. My mother had been working with a moving company in Wichita, making her transition back to Finch Warehousing & Transfer much easier. She had stayed in touch with the family, which included H. L. "Sonny" Callahan, her first cousin.

Sonny was one of nine children. He was very close to my grandparents and had come to live with them at the age of twelve or so. Sonny and Mom were particularly close and both considered their relationship as brother and sister. He had grown up in the family business until he enlisted in the U.S. Navy. Sometime after he left military service, he returned to Finch Warehousing & Transfer and was employed in various capacities. According to my mother, he had not been happy there and had accepted a job with Scott Paper Company. This was immediately before my grandfather's death, and he assured my mother that he hadn't told my grandfather he was leaving the company. Before Sonny could leave, my grandfather died; obviously, that changed his plans and the company appointed him president.

Mr. Pat Myers was the vice president for the company, and my mother told us that he was offered the presidency first but turned it down in deference to Sonny. My grandmother was also in favor of this arrangement. My mother was asked to come aboard and handle the household moving claims, which was part of her expertise with her previous employers. My father would later come aboard part-time, while he was serving in the air force. He would be the operations manager for the parts of the moving division which were working along the Allied Van Lines affiliation. For the military moving bids, we were allowed to represent more than one major moving company. For example, in addition to Allied Van Lines, we represented Atlas Van Lines.

Chapter Two

Players in the Game
and Rules of Operation

In the midseventies, clearly 70 to 80 percent of our business was with Scott Paper Company. Their plant was within just a few miles of our warehouses. We handled their paper products in various stages of production: from pulp to roll product to finished case products.

When I joined Finch after graduating from the University of Alabama in 1978, I actually had an informal interview with Sonny for my future with the company. Sonny said that I would begin as a clerk under our warehousing operations manager, who would also train me. What I didn't realize at the time was the resentment of me by that manager and some of the supervisors, which I guess was understandable. They probably felt the "bosses' kid" thought he was coming in and would impose his "college-boy" theories to their hands-on, veteran ways. I really underestimated this at the beginning.

For example, I had developed a detailed work measurement tool for the warehousing division, which required timely input from the supervisors. After a few weeks of getting incomplete reports from them, I complained to our manager. He said he would take care of the problem immediately. When it hadn't improved, I asked one of the supervisors what was going on...Why weren't they giving me the data? The supervisor said that the manager told them to ignore the requests because they seemed unimportant.

I went directly to Sonny, who had asked me to put the reports together in the first place, and asked for a quick meeting with the manager and him. I knew that Sonny was more of a hands-off manager, but I was really ticked off and wanted this sorted out. I told Sonny at that meeting that I was having trouble getting the data because the manager told the supervisors to ignore my requests. I don't know who was more flustered, our manager or Sonny; Sonny hated this kind of confrontation. But from that point on, I had no trouble getting the information I needed.

This was just the beginning of my understanding the breakdown of communication in our company. Rather than dealing with issues in an open and productive way, Sonny would do everything he could to avoid any conflict. In the future, this weakness would prove to be the ultimate enemy and fuel for the eventual feud.

One of our three supervisors in the warehousing division at that time would become a key leader in the future of the Finch Companies. Bruce Byrd, who had started as a forklift operator, showed a lot of initiative and willingness to improve himself and the company. He was someone whose judgment I would depend on in the difficult years to come.

Our other main emphasis was the household goods moving and storage business. We were agents for Allied Van Lines, with offices in Mobile, Birmingham, and Montgomery. My father, S. C. "Sam" Fulton, managed the household goods division along with my mother, Betty Jo, who handled the claims as her main duty, among various other tasks. My brother, Danny, was also employed in this area of the company. My uncle and aunt, Phil and Geraldine Barnhart, had run our Birmingham moving division. The company closed this division in the early eighties. For a short period of time, Scott Callahan, Sonny's oldest son, worked in sales for this division. In addition, Scott began working for the other warehousing entity set up by Sonny, among other investors, which was Great Southern Company.

Overview of the Companies

1. This is the main building which housed the moving company, the administrative division, and some warehousing operations. The foreground portion was the original building, which was built by Thomas W. Finch in 1955. The smaller portion was added onto the original building in the mid-1960s, making it about 80,000 square feet overall.

2. Also in the mid-60s, the Finch building was constructed for our warehousing operations and consisted of approximately 85,000 square feet.

3. Building #3 was completed in 1969 by Sonny and some outside partners. Nobody from the Finch or Fulton families was involved in this venture. It was a separate corporation called Great Southern. Eventually, in the process of consolidation in 1984, this was rolled into the Finch Companies. When it was built, it housed a warehousing account with Scott Paper, who was already doing business with Finch. This was a 100,000-square-foot building.

4. This building was built and used under contract to Union Carbide for ten years beginning in 1975. After that period, we took over the building and used it for warehousing activity. We eventually

named the building the Fulton building. It was 100,000 square feet of space.

5. The Fincraft building was completed in 1977 and housed 100,000 square feet of warehousing accounts.

6. The Callahan building was completed in 1978 and housed 150,000 square feet of warehousing accounts.

7. (not shown) Our Furniture Leasing Concepts division began in the seventies with just a few apartments worth of furniture and grew steadily over the years. By 1984, we had built a showroom and warehouse on Azalea Road for the furniture leasing business, which was run by my mother.

Chapter Three
The Political Playing Field

S onny got his political training early with his involvement in the Mobile Jaycees. He told me that it was the
best education he had received in preparation for his
future endeavors.

Mobile is now, and has always been, a politically conservative community. In the late sixties and early seventies, there was,
for all practical purposes, only one party in Alabama—the Alabama Democratic Party. This was not to be confused with the
national Democrats who distinguished themselves with a don-
key as their logo. Alabama Democrats use a rooster as their logo,
and were frequently at political odds with the national Democratic party. Alabama strongly supported Republican candidate
Barry Goldwater for president in 1964 against Lyndon Johnson,
the Democratic candidate.

That same year, Sonny's close friend Jack Edwards was swept
into the U.S. Congress as a Republican from the First Congressional District, largely on Goldwater's coattails. Almost no Republicans were elected to local or state offices.

When Sonny became president of our company in 1964,
Brookley Air Force Base, which was located in Mobile, provid-

ed a substantial portion of our moving business. Even with the news that the base was scheduled to close, the moving business enjoyed some of its best years thanks to the transfer of those 15,000 families from the Mobile area.

During this period, Sonny spoke to numerous groups and civic organizations to solicit moving business and began to develop an interest in politics. In 1970, with the blessing and support of Genevieve Finch and the Fultons, Sonny ran for and won a seat in the Alabama House of Representatives as a "rooster" Democrat. All of us supported his bid and worked toward its success. Back then, the legislature only met every other year, so the family felt that his time away from the business would not be a detriment. Sonny was reelected in 1974, and in 1978 was elected easily to the Alabama Senate.

By this time, the Alabama legislature was meeting annually and Sonny was deeply entrenched in politics. He had gone from a part-time to a full-time politician, and he rarely spent more than a half-day or so on Mondays and Fridays in the Finch office. At the end of his first term in the Senate, Sonny decided to run for lieutenant governor in 1982. It was rare for someone from our part of the state to be elected in a statewide office at that time, but Sonny wanted to try it.

He campaigned tirelessly across the state, but in the end was defeated handily in the Democratic primary. Sonny was very hurt and stayed away from the office for most of several months after the bitter defeat. He eventually did return to the company on a more-or-less full-time basis, but this was not to last very long.

I had graduated from the University of Alabama in August of 1978 and immediately went to work for our company. By then, Sonny was very involved in his political life and I was placed on a fast track to learn and develop skills in the management of the company. By the time of his lieutenant–gubernatorial defeat, I was much more deeply involved in day to day operations of the company than was Sonny, and I was becoming more and more looked upon as an obvious successor to him as president.

Indeed, in early 1983, our Republican congressman Jack Edwards told insiders that he would not seek reelection in 1984. I discussed this with Sonny, and he told me that Edwards had approached him, suggested that he switch parties, and run for the vacancy as a Republican. He also told me that were he to run, and be elected, it would be necessary for him to resign as president of Finch.

I felt sure that Sonny would do well to make the switch. Indeed, he had supported the candidacy of Ronald Reagan for president in 1980 as one of the "Democrats for Reagan." When he made his decision to switch and run, he asked me to be his campaign chairman, which I was honored and pleased to do. As fate would have it, I had already become involved with the Alabama Young Republicans, among other civic activities. Sonny and I agreed, however, that my primary duties would be running the company.

When Sonny announced that he would be running for Congress as a Republican, I was a member of the Mobile County Republican Executive Committee. The members of that committee did not exactly break down the door with enthusiasm for his announcement. Furthermore, the chairman of the committee announced that he would also be running for the party's nomination. The chairman's camp went negative quickly, attempting to connect Sonny with local Democratic officeholders who would eventually end up in prison for corruption in office.

The Democratic primary featured an interesting battle between a well-known school board member and a local attorney. The board member was actually a friend of Sonny, but he was also a lightning rod for controversy as an outspoken critic of the Mobile School Board of Education and most of his colleagues on the school board. The attorney was an honest, well-spoken, noncontroversial conservative Democrat, which served him well in defeating the school board member in the primary.

The Republican primary was interesting in that the "establishment" Republicans, those who had been supporting Republicans in the trenches for many, many unsuccessful years, resented the movement of former Democrats into the party. After all, they had struggled all of those years, and now that Ronald Reagan had made it ok to be Republican, they weren't just going to move aside. Several of my fellow county committee members ranted and raved at the monthly meetings in opposition to Sonny, much of it coming from the county chairman who was a candidate himself.

After several sessions of listening to several members beating up Sonny, including rants from the chairman, I had reached my limit. I asked for the floor and began an impassioned defense of Sonny, whom most of them knew personally. I proudly reviewed his public service record, as well as what I knew of his personal character. I also reminded the committee of his support for Reagan in the last presidential election and that many of them had chastised me in years past for not getting Sonny to switch parties.

I received surprising applause at the end of my little speech, and even got congratulations from the chairman after the meeting. I'm not sure Sonny ever knew of my going to bat for him in such extremes; he never mentioned it to me.

Sonny won the Republican primary and devoted virtually all of his time during the ensuing months to running against his Democratic opponent. Sonny won that race as well. Thereafter, in January 1985, he resigned as president of the company but remained as chairman of the board of directors.

Chapter Four
My Beginning as Finch President

The company I was about to take over would be struc-
tured quite differently than the previous setup. Before
March 1, 1985, our companies were set up as four different C Corporations: Finch Warehousing & Transfer, Finch
Realty, Great Southern Corporation, and Furniture Leasing
Concepts (FLC). While ownership was different in all of them,
the two main shareholders agreed that all four companies would
be combined into one S Corporation, owned 51 percent by the
Fulton family and 49 percent by the Callahan family. This decision was primarily based upon the tax advantages which came
from the S Corp status. It was a dramatic restructuring of the
business, but legal advice was not sought before the agreement
was reached.

In the years prior to this change, it was the practice of the
shareholders of Finch Warehousing & Transfer to declare bonus-
es to themselves for virtually 100 percent of any profits, mainly
to avoid the double taxation inherent in C Corps. Also, on the
books, Finch Realty would act as landlord, owning the land and
buildings, and therefore charging rent to the operating divisions.
Furniture Leasing Concepts operated separately from the other

companies. Great Southern Corporation consisted of one building, a 100,000 square-foot operation, which was located contiguously to the other five buildings on Finch property.

By the time this transformation occurred, all of the non-family partners had been bought out so that the only people left were from either the Fulton or Callahan families. These changes made financial comparisons with previous years very difficult. At least since Sonny had become president, the companies were run chiefly to provide income to the families.

I was thrilled with the opportunity given to me and wanted to run the company as professionally as possible. I also thought that we should tighten up some of the perks that had been in place for family members. This included things like using employees to do non-company-related errands, paying for gas for family members and others, many of whom didn't even work there. I also felt that with the sub-S setup, our financial records would be more transparent and I wanted to monitor the health of the "whole" company. For at least a decade or more prior to that time, we didn't even have a monthly balance sheet to look at...this was only seen after the yearly audit. Sonny told me we didn't need one...he knew what we had.

For the first couple of years, there seemed to be very few disagreements between Sonny and me. The first four or five months included monthly meetings with Sonny and me, so that we could go over the P&Ls and discuss the results.

We set up our P&Ls with separate divisions in the following manner:

Branch 1 – Mobile Household Goods
Branch 2 – Main Warehouse Building
Branch 3 – Finch Warehouse Building
Branch 4 – Great Southern Warehouse Building
Branch 5 – Montgomery Warehouse Building
Branch 6 – Administrative Division
Branch 7 – Local Drayage Division
Branch 8 – Fincraft Warehouse Division
Branch 9 – Callahan Warehouse Division
Branch 10 – Fulton Warehouse Division
Branch 11 – Furniture Leasing Concepts Division
Branch 12 – Finch Realty

This was an example of how we unnecessarily complicated our bookkeeping with divisional segregation (that sounds ridiculous in itself). Every expense had to be divided up in some manner to try to match the proper division. The ridiculous part of it was that the warehousing divisions did not operate separately. Nevertheless, it did lead to some humorous juggling when Sonny questioned our operations manager about the individual warehousing operations.

Sonny would ask him why Branch 2 was not doing as well as Branch 3, and why Branch 8 was not as productive as Branch 9. Our operations manager would get all flustered and begin sending inbound shipments to the "non-performing" buildings, which would precipitate a new round of questions...it was like squeezing a balloon. Sonny questioned me in the same manner when I took over, but I tried to explain to him that the warehouses operated in the most effective and efficient manner based on the customers' product needs and our operating procedures, but I guess he chose not to look at it this way. It simply made no difference, in reality, whether an individual building performed better than another did. It made more sense to look at the bottom line in all six of the warehousing operations. In our future disagreements, this method of analysis only led to frustration on both our parts.

The first few years were exciting, and profitable. In fact, we made record profits. We were also heavily laden with debt. This was the early to mid-eighties and it seemed that growth by indebtedness was the norm for most businesses. Savings and loan companies were lending at record rates. Interest rates were still high, but had come down from the seventies. Sonny believed, and stated to me several times, that "leverage" was the way to go. Using as little of your own money was the best way to manage a growing company. Our first disagreement came when the renewal on our loans came up and he encouraged me to maximize the loan amount. Inflation was an ally in this strategy, because the loan value of the collateral, our buildings, increased regularly without any real physical improvements. One of our buildings, the Fulton Building, had a few hundred thousand dollars in equity, which had not been tied up as loan collateral. All I wanted to do was renew the current debt, at its existing level. He insisted that we maximize our leverage by borrowing as much as the bank would let us.

Another area of frustration came from Sonny's original insistence that I not be allowed to spend more than $5,000 without his approval. I tried to stick with this for the first six to eight months, but it became very cumbersome as time went by. I called Sonny often to let him know what I was doing, without even a single objection for the first several months. Eventually, I told him that it seemed unnecessary, and that I was hoping he would remove this limitation...after all, I was managing a company with more than $2.7 million in yearly revenue. I was involved in all of the day-to-day decision-making, and Sonny had not really been involved on a front-line basis for years. As controversial as the removal of this restriction would become later, he agreed without any fanfare when I asked him.

Overall, though, Sonny seemed happy with what we were doing. We had shown our largest customer that we were providing measurable improvement in service to them, which they rewarded with substantial increases in business. We had implemented quality procedures and better training for our employees. I'd like to take credit for all of the growth which was to come to us in the mid to late eighties, but realistically, it had as much to do with the demand from the paper industry as anything else. I will say that our top management people, especially Bruce Byrd and Jerry McCoy, had a lot to do with the increase in confidence of performance.

Most importantly, we improved the profits of the companies to all-time highs, including the aggregate predecessor companies. At least to most onlookers, things had never seemed better. During this period, Sonny had put together a group of key supporters from his congressional district that he designated as his finance committee. This group met on a regular basis at the International Trade Club in Mobile to get updates on things going on in Washington. I had been invited to all of these meetings for the first few years, and I loved going. I have always been fascinated with how things work in Congress. Sonny's brother, George Callahan, even joked that the company was doing so well that we couldn't afford to have Sonny lose his seat in Congress. Sonny just laughed along with everyone else.

Election season came in 1986, and Sonny found himself unopposed, as often happened in a non-presidential campaign year. The company was moving along quite well, as was my own career. I had become even more involved in the Jaycees and had the opportunity to run for president of the Alabama Jaycees in May 1986. Even though I had no opposition, I wanted to travel the state of Alabama and visit our members in their hometowns. We had more than 110 chapters with more than 5,000 members throughout the state. I had the support of my wife, Lane, who was pregnant with our third child. We had two daughters, Chandler Marie, born in 1982, and Ashley Lane, who was born in 1984. Lane made a lot of sacrifices for me, knowing that my duties would be very time-consuming and require a lot of statewide travel. I also had Sonny's support and encouragement, as well as the rest of our family.

My election took place in Florence, Alabama, one week after the birth of our son, Thomas Finch Fulton. It was one of the most exciting and rewarding years of my life. I traveled throughout the state and spoke more than sixty times, in large and small chapters. Most of my travel was weekend-related, but there were many times during the week that I was gone. This was also during the more profitable times for the Finch Companies. There were so many personally rewarding moments for me that year. Nevertheless, the challenges of that year changed me for the rest of my life.

Chapter Five
Rumblings in the Background

For years under Sonny's leadership, we had systematically allowed 100 percent of our profits to be declared as dividends each year. This practice seemed a little loose to me, but it was entrenched. We didn't even discuss this procedure in the board meetings. It just seemed to happen. However, even though we were making record profits, we were getting a little tight on cash flow. A major contributor to this problem was that, in addition to declaring 100 percent dividends, we were lending cash to Sonny over and above his dividends, so that his debt to the company was in excess of $137,000 at the end of 1987. He simply sent dozens of his bills to Dan Miller, our bookkeeper, and told him to charge his company account. Eventually, Dan seemed very concerned about this and suggested that we should limit these disbursements. We made an agreement with Sonny that he would limit his draws to $10,000 per month. As an afterthought, he said in the meeting, "Of course, you'll need to forward to me an additional amount for quarterly tax payments," which he said would be about $30,000 per quarter.

That was not my intention, but we reluctantly agreed to it in that meeting. This actually raised the amount of his cash outlay to $240,000 a year. Sometime after that, I began discussing with him the need for that to be decreased, so that the company would have money to operate and improve facilities. Gene Gibbons, our company CPA and auditor, said that Sonny's debt should be acknowledged with a signed note to the company each year. Each year he said that he presented this note to Sonny with instructions to sign, and each year Sonny simply ignored him. Neither Sonny nor Gene ever told us why Sonny didn't sign.

Toward the end of 1987, Sonny introduced the subject of our buying him out of the company. It seemed like a reasonable idea, since he had not been involved in any of the operations of the company and was draining cash from our operations. Even though we were making record profits up until then, he was not particularly interested with future involvement. I know that the time he spent as a congressman was very time consuming.

The first notion of our selling the company was raised in 1983 or 1984. Leaseway[1] had approached the company about buying us out, and we listened to what they had to say regarding a buy-out of all of our stock. Sonny told us that he felt we could net around $4 million for the company, and after the company's debt was paid off from the proceeds, each family would have about $2 million left.

Sonny was so pleased with the prospect of receiving $2 million for his share of the company that he encouraged us to go along with such an arrangement. However, Leaseway told us later that, after examining our records, they were only interested in paying off the debt of the company and were shocked that Sonny was insisting on so much more.

In 1987, Sonny asked us to buy him out; and without much fanfare, he asked the company to pay our corporate attorney, Tom Hudson, to negotiate "price" for his benefit, while Charles Chamblee, my mother's accountant, would represent our side also at the company's expense. He said that this would keep

---

1   Leaseway was primarily a trucking operation which had begun buying warehousing facilities throughout the country in an effort to diversify their supply-chain services.

us from arguing with each other regarding the buyout amount. It seemed reasonable to me. I wrote a letter to Hudson stating that we authorized him to negotiate a purchase price for Sonny's shares in the company. At this point, the buyout seemed to be on friendly terms. What was really happening in the background was much more devious.

First, Sonny wanted to enter into binding arbitration, whereby an offer to sell constitutes an offer to buy. We were most definitely not in favor of that route, since we were not interested at all in selling out to him. Tom Hudson "reluctantly" agreed to make an offer. Sonny's attorney, in a letter dated March 15, 1988, began to set up a premise that if we didn't accept his offer, we would be hard-pressed to curtail the present payments being loaned to Sonny, along with declaring 100 percent of the yearly profits. Hudson wrote that they had tried to "find a generalized amicable method, without the necessity of hard negotiations, to work the matter out." We did not see this letter until much later.

In a letter dated April 20, 1988, Tom Hudson sent a proposal to Charles Chamblee, our representative for the buyout of Sonny's interests. It was a nine-page analysis which unfortunately was fatally flawed on the first page. Hudson's first approach was to use a "Capitalized Income from Operations" method. Hudson was not using the "audited" Total Operating Revenues, and therefore included as revenue the internal rents from our "Realty" or "Holding" division, which was charged to the operating divisions. The auditors would adjust these figures at the end of the year to show the real figures. This miscalculation artificially inflated Hudson's valuation by more than $7.3 million overall, or $3.6 million for Sonny's undiscounted minority shares.

His second approach was the "Net Asset Value" approach. His first mistake was to value the buildings at insured value, rather than market value or depreciated value. He also mistakenly stated that the buildings were insured at 80 percent of their replacement value when they were actually insured at 100 percent of replacement value. Then he placed an increasing value equal to the Consumer Price Index for the years 1985, 1986, and 1987. Furthermore, he used a value for the land based on an offer for the purchase of one of our six buildings, which we never consummated, and extrapolated that to a value of $292,500. These were just some of the fallacies of Hudson's work, all of which were pointed out to us in a letter from David Park, an accountant from Ernst & Young, in his evaluation of this approach.

Chapter Six
New Ventures

The late eighties were a very important time in the growth of The Finch Companies. Scott Paper Company approached us about expanding our trucking service to long-haul, truckload ability. We had developed a true partnership with Scott Paper and we felt that it was worth a try, given their substantial support and encouragement. I also believed that we needed that kind of diversity to avoid having all of our growth tied up in the buildings. I presented the trucking division proposal to the full board at the directors' meeting in January 1988. There was virtually no opposition to the idea. Sonny asked what our loss exposure was in this venture, and I told him that we hoped it would not be a loss, but that we didn't feel it would lose more than $50,000.

Bruce Byrd and I were very excited about the growth possibilities of the trucking expansion and went about our due diligence on how to make it as successful as possible. Not only were we excited about the trucking part of the business, we also felt it would be the vehicle that would allow us to expand into other cities. We had talked to other warehousing companies who used the trucking business to develop corridors which opened up opportunities for warehousing at both ends. We were very successful in warehousing and additionally, our current trucking business already contributed to additional warehouse business. It seemed like the perfect synergy.

One of the decisions we made was to lease our equipment, five tractors and eight trailers, to begin this division. Our CPA, Gene Gibbons, advised us that there was no major advantage of purchasing over leasing, and in fact, it would be easier to obtain leases than financing. Therefore, we took that direction. We started the trucking division in July 1988. We owned a set of truck scales at our main warehouse, which we used to weigh our own Allied Van Lines trucks as well as all kinds of freight hauler trucks. When those drivers came in, we would quiz them about everything from where they felt the business was going, to how they were compensated, as well as any other intelligence we could gather. In addition, we found out what the prevailing wage and benefit structure was in our area, so that we could position ourselves as a better-than-average carrier for drivers. At that time, one of the biggest challenges for trucking companies was the recruiting and retaining of highly qualified drivers.

We tried to estimate the revenue and expenses as accurately as possible, so that we could present some sort of budget or pro-forma statements to our board. Our board consisted of all family members: my mother, my father, my brother, Scott Callahan and Sonny Callahan, and me. The first projection I gave to the board, in January 1988, showed a small profit of around $37,000 at the end of the year. Unfortunately, the actual figures showed a loss of about $26,000. (This actual number would become a major factor in later discussions and court proceedings.)

Sonny was preparing for his first contested re-election effort since he was elected to Congress. His opponent was John Tyson Jr., who was to become Mobile's district attorney in later years. I remembered John from a debate with him years before at a local high school. I was president of the Young Republicans prior to the Reagan-Carter election. John represented Jimmy Carter and

I represented Ronald Reagan. I was petrified and actually took a day off of work to prepare for the event. I really hadn't done much public speaking at that time, and I knew John had been very active politically. It ended up as a no-contest, not because of any exhibition of debating skill on my part, but because the audience was very pro-Reagan. All John could say was that Jimmy Carter was a good ole Southern boy and that should be enough. They didn't buy it.

I was excited about getting involved in Sonny's campaign in 1988. I called Sonny's office and told his campaign manager that I was ready, willing, and able to get going. I was taken aback, to say the least, when I was told I wouldn't be needed...they were only using paid staff for this election. I called Sonny and told him what had happened and that I didn't understand why I wasn't going to be involved. He repeated the same thing about no volunteer staff for that election. I wondered if there wasn't some underlying reason I was not wanted in Sonny's campaign. In the election, Sonny easily defeated Tyson 59 to 41 percent.

Instead of Sonny's campaign, I got involved as Jack Kemp's 1st Congressional District Chairman in his campaign for president. I am pretty sure I was recommended to him by Sonny, but I don't know that for a fact. I was, and still am, a huge fan of Jack Kemp and his ideas of tax reform and entrepreneurship. It gave me the opportunity to meet with him several times in person.

In the meantime, since we summarily rejected Sonny's offer from Tom Hudson, they asked us to come up with a counteroffer. I sent a letter to Tom Hudson on July 7, 1988 [see Appendix One] in which we countered Callahan's ridiculous $3.8 million offer. First, we showed him what he could expect to receive in the unlikely scenario that we continued to drain our treasury by declaring all of our profits as dividends. If we assumed a return of 10 percent to ten years of those payments, the present value of that stream of payments would be just over $620,000. Even with that consideration, we offered him $1 million for his shares in the company.

Hudson summarily rejected our offer in a letter dated August 1, 1988 [see Appendix Two]. He argued that if Sonny's minority ownership was valued at $3.5 million, then we must be under-utilizing the assets if we are only willing to pay $1 million. We found it incredible that these were the same assets that Callahan managed for twenty years. When he tried to sell those same assets before my presidency began, Leaseway rebuffed his "valu-ation" of $2 million for his shares. In fact, they valued it at less than zero. Hudson made the point that their offer to sell would be an offer to buy at the same price. He knew very well that we had absolutely no desire to sell…at any price.

The purpose of my offer was to demonstrate to him that should he remain a shareholder, and under the most generous arrangements, he should not expect to receive more than my examples for the next ten years. In fact, he received more in pay and dividends during the first five years of my presidency than he did in the last five years of his presidency. Since we were a C Corporation during his tenure, it was his practice to virtually bonus to the shareholders/directors the vast majority, if not all, of the profits of the companies, in order to minimize any taxes due from the corporation.

Because of this, there was never much cash left in the com-pany for things like maintenance and capital improvement of the infrastructure. In fact, when he was running for Congress, and had professionals advising him of ways to be bought out, they all stated that the company was virtually fully leveraged and cash poor at the time I was to take over. It was always Sonny's prac-tice to borrow against any equity that inflation might give to the warehouse buildings.

Furthermore, Hudson criticized our intention to stop the draining of the company's cash, which had been grossly in favor of Callahan and much to my mother's detriment. The company owed her hundreds of thousands of dollars, which were not paid to her because Sonny had been given substantial loans from the company. Our bankers, CPA, bookkeeper, and virtually anyone who saw our situation deemed it ridiculous. Our CPA, who was a close ally of Sonny, made that point time after time. We even challenged him to show us anyone who would advise us to continue Sonny's way. To this day, no one has come forward to recommend his way.

The fact that Hudson misused key figures in Sonny's original offer never seemed to faze him. He just ignored that, and even though his letter says he would make the "appropriate adjustments," he never did. In addition to using inappropriate methodology, Hudson made no allowance for two discounting methods that are frequently used when valuing a minority shareholder's value in a closely held company. Most valuation experts discount a minority interest by around 25 percent, and further discount similarly for lack of marketability.

One of the key tenets of the law in Alabama is that the majority is not required to buy out the stock of the minority. Our attorneys assured us that we had to be fair, but that we are not required to purchase, no matter how much pressure is applied. In the next few years, Sonny made every effort possible to do that very thing. We felt at this time that the gap between the offers was huge and would not be closed anytime soon.

With that in mind, on August 9, 1988, I wrote Hudson, thanking him for his efforts and terminating his services, which had been paid for by the company [see Appendix Three].

For the Finch Companies, 1988 was an improved year for cash flow. Because of that, we wanted to put our extra cash to work for us and decided to put some of it into some State Docks bonds and some stocks. For the first several months, our investments seemed to be working great for us, with results of more than $20,000 to the positive. One of the duties I had as president was to maximize return on our funds, and that is what I was attempting to do. We wanted to make sure that the money was available for operations and for capital improvements to our mostly metal warehouse buildings.

The investing was done openly and everyone in our office knew what we were doing. However, since Sonny rarely contacted me or anyone else in the company, he was not aware of it. In retrospect, I should have made an active effort to let him know what we were doing. I incorrectly assumed that Sonny's son Scott was keeping him informed. I eventually surmised that they weren't even talking about what was going on at Finch. Ultimately, we ended up losing only about $70, but I unwisely let Morgan-Keegan talk me into leveraging margin accounts and investing in more risky stocks than I should have. One particular stock, Miniscribe, was doctoring their books and ended up almost single-handedly losing all of our gains.

It had been an exciting and very positive year, and I want to brag about all of those positive things that were going on. In the past, especially before I took over as president, board meetings were only fifteen-minute get-togethers, with the minutes written up later only as a formality. I was going to change that. I spent days and days preparing as many charts and graphs and spreadsheets as I could so we could go over everything in detail. I planned for the meeting to start at five o'clock on Monday, January 30, 1989, which would include sandwiches brought in so we wouldn't need to break for supper. I had anticipated about two to three hours to wrap up the whole thing. I presented every division in detail for each month of the year. That's thirteen divisions...in detail. This turned out to play perfectly into Sonny's strategy.

We had developed a document for each major division based on planning guides used by Jaycee chapters to set goals and expectations. We presented these at the board meeting for the household moving divisions as well as detailed financial statements for each major division. After we had gone through all of this, Sonny started questioning almost every item in every report. Some of the questions were so nonsensical as to be unanswerable.

For example, he would ask, "If depreciation expense in Branch 2 for August was 'x,' what would you expect the depreciation to be next year in August for that same branch?"

This went on for hours and hours. When I prepared for this meeting, I had only gotten about three hours of sleep the night before; and after hours of Sonny's haranguing, tempers began to flare and I even had my father mad at me at one point. It was truly one of the craziest meetings I've ever seen. We adjourned the meeting at around midnight and scheduled to reconvene on February 27, 1989. My brother, Danny, lived across the street from me. When we got home after that meeting, we stayed up and discussed how flabbergasted we were with what had occurred in the previous seven hours.

During that January board meeting, Sonny made several references to the undeclared dividends, or what accountants call the accumulated adjustments account. I asked Steve Mixon, with Ernst & Whinney (now known as Ernst & Young) to educate me on these "AA" accounts. Sonny constantly stated that any undeclared dividends were the property of the individual shareholders and, therefore, we had no right to withhold those funds.

Steve's letter reads as follows:

Dear Tommy:

You have asked us to discuss the earnings accumulated by an S corporation as they relate to the individual shareholders of that S corporation.

The AA account represents all the earnings of the corporation accumulated during S corporation years that has been taxed to the shareholders, less any amounts distributed to shareholders. The AA account is listed on Schedule M of Form 1120S but is not broken down by shareholder nor is it shown on the individual K-1's. Generally, to the extent of a positive balance in AA account, the corporation can make pro rata tax-free distributions to its shareholders if the board of directors decides to declare a dividend distribution.

The Bureau of National Affairs, Inc., in its Tax Management Portfolio on S Corporations states, "The AA account, like its predecessor in PTI (previously taxed income), *cannot be directly transferred from one shareholder to another.* However, it is a *corporate level account much like accumulated earnings and profits.* Thus, unlike PTI, the AA account left by a terminating shareholder is available for distribution to remaining shareholders; it is not lost even though it is not directly transferable." Therefore, the AA account is not the personal property of the S corporation's shareholders even though they have been taxed on the corporate income accumulated in the AA account.

If you have any questions, please do not hesitate to call me.

Very truly yours,
Stephen W. Mixon
Partner
(emphasis added)

This letter is one example of a key element in this story. It would be taken totally out of context in the future. I also have a letter from our attorney meant to further clarify Sonny's assertions that the company is required by law to distribute each year as a dividend 100 percent of the net earnings, because the company has elected to be taxed as an S Corporation for income tax purposes. In this letter from Watson Smith, he summarizes it in this way:

...In summary, the corporate law in Alabama is very clear that in the absence of any provision in the corporate charter or by-laws and in the absence of any agreement between the shareholders and the corporation, the declaration of dividends is a matter for the discretion of the board of directors with which a court of equity will not interfere in the absence of funds. Therefore, if the Board of Directors of the Company has valid business reasons for retaining a portion of the net earnings of the Company for corporate purposes, then an Alabama court should not overrule the business judgment of the Board of Directors.

The mere fact that the Company has elected to be taxed as an
S Corporation should not change this result, inasmuch as said
election merely affects the tax treatment of the Company and
its shareholders and is a matter of tax law rather than corporate
law...

I wanted to be sure that we had expert advice before attempting another wild board meeting like the one we had just experienced. I was kidding myself—the February continuance of the January board meeting was even more bizarre. The meeting opened with Sonny using a tape recorder. This meeting lasted three hours with virtually nothing of note accomplished. We attempted to present some resolutions at this meeting, but the whole thing degenerated and the meeting was adjourned. We wouldn't get together again until May 26, 1989.

Chapter Seven
Open Hostilities

I f we had thought the two previous attempts at concluding the board meeting were strange, the May meeting took the prize. We had put together five resolutions, with the help and advice of our attorneys, in order to clarify some questions Sonny had brought up at the other meetings. Even though we had experienced good profits over the last few years, our cash flow was anemic. We were attempting to refinance much of our debt, so much of which was on short terms.

Additionally, we had been lending Sonny substantial amounts, over and above his dividends. Even though we had tried to slow these down, he had fought us every step of the way. I mentioned before that he had agreed to "limit" his draws to $10,000 per month plus approximately $30,000 per quarter for taxes. I had discussed further limitations on Sonny's loans on several occasions, including a meeting at his house. In addition to the loan limitations, I had been advised by several people that continuing to declare 100 percent of profits as dividends was unwise. These included our bankers, our CPA, attorneys, and others. Since Sonny was unwilling to agree with any of this advice, we decided to formalize these changes through board resolutions. The first resolution addressed these concerns. We declared dividends in two areas of income. As agents for Allied Van Lines, and shareholders, we had received about $250,000 in proceeds from the sale of our Allied stock to National Freight Consortium. We declared 100 percent dividend on these proceeds. We also declared a dividend of 50 percent on the profits from the ordinary operations of the company.

Since it was already May 1989, we ratified the loans already given to Sonny in the amount of $80,000 for the first five months of that year. We also agreed to lend quarterly tax payments to Sonny, based on actual quarterly profits at the level of 36 percent of 48.9 percent (Sonny's ownership). He had always complained that he was having to pay taxes on profits he wasn't going to receive...this took care of that concern.

The key part of this resolution, though, was the following:

Beginning June 1989, the only continuing loans will be those made to cover the tax liabilities of the stockholders based on actual quarterly profits...

Before the declaration of dividends made during this meeting, Sonny owed the Finch Companies more than $450,000. The dividend reduced his debt to just over $280,000. On the other hand, the company owed my mother more than $200,000 because we were unable to pay her from the remaining cash flow.

Sonny had also sent a letter to our banker, which seemed reasonable on its face. On February 3, 1989, he wrote a letter to AmSouth Bank which read as follows:

Gentlemen:

I am pleased that since I commenced representing our District in Congress, Finch Companies, Inc. have continued to be profitable. I am attempting to closely follow their business activities and also fulfill the duties of public office.

On behalf of The Finch Companies, I executed, personally and individually, as guarantor, a Continuing Guaranty Agreement with your bank as well as appropriate corporate resolution on behalf of The Continuing Guaranty Agreement provides that it shall extend to extensions or renewals of any existing indebtedness [sic]. It also provides that it will apply to new loans and advances.

Now that I am not involved on a day by day basis in the management of the company, I would appreciate having notice from you of any proposed new loan or indebtedness sought by The Finch Companies, Inc. prior to any advance being made on that new loan. Simply as a matter of good business practice, it will be necessary for me to give to you my express approval for any such new loan or indebtedness prior to my being held responsible for that loan or indebtedness under the guaranty...

This letter sounds very reasonable on its face, and I certainly had no quarrel with what it said. The only exception would be with respect to his efforts to "closely follow their business activities." We had rarely seen him over the past four years, except for the board meetings. What I found out much later was that he had discussed my leadership of the company in very harsh terms, by phone and at least on one occasion in person.

I know it's almost never done, but Danny and I sent a letter to AmSouth on March 3, 1989, asking the bank to consider the removal of Sonny's name from the Continuing Guaranty Agreement. We were not able to convince the bank, even though they privately acknowledged that Sonny's only viable asset was the stock in the company, and even that was highly leveraged. I'm sure it didn't hurt that he was a U.S. congressman.

Because of these communications with the bank and the concern from Sonny, we also passed resolutions ratifying trans-actions we had made with other banks and equipment leasing entities, even though there was no extension of Sonny's personal guaranties. We also authorized more flexibility in borrowing for me as president, and my mother as secretary. We were beginning to suspect that Sonny may be blocking our efforts to improve our financing picture behind the scenes.

After we passed the resolutions in the May 1989 meeting, we went on to discuss the various divisions and their operating results for 1988. The company made an overall profit of almost $500,000, of which $250,000 came from the extraordinary in-come from the sale of the Allied Van Lines stock. The operating profit was down from the previous year, due mainly to losses in the moving divisions and the new trucking division. However, it was still a healthy profit. Unfortunately, we were desperately short on cash. There were several reasons for that, but the most obvious one was that we had distributed more than $537,000 to the shareholders in 1988. Our working capital decreased by more than $280,000 that year. No wonder we were having so much trouble making our payments as timely as we needed.

The meeting included discussion regarding the motion to "limit loans to shareholders to zero, except for those loans given to all shareholders for the purpose of paying quarterly tax esti-mates, by June 1989."

After I received that motion, and a second, I said, "Is there any discussion?"

Sonny said, "Yeah, I'd like to discuss it too, to say that, natu-rally I object. You know, I can't live on zero income, but you tell me that y'all have met already and you've agreed on it, so I'm not gonna change any minds. But, it just says in June, 1989…is that in perpetuity?"

I said, "Until the board changes it."

"Well, couldn't we limit it to the year 1989, or until the next meeting of the board…By cashing in my retirement system, I could live until January 1990. But after that, I would be in sad shape," Sonny argued.

After a few more minutes of discussion, Sonny tried to elicit sympathy from Mom and Dad. "He's saying that from now on," he said, referring to me, "I won't be able to draw any money from the company and I'm asking if that's in perpetuity, or in pleading with you all to make it just for the balance of this year with the hopes that maybe you all will understand that I can't live on zero income. And that, next year, maybe additional loans will be granted to me based on some percentage of profit, or something."

After more discussion, I responded, "I fully expect that every year, a motion would be allowed to come up to bring up a change."

Sonny replied, "I understand, but I still think it ought to be forced onto the agenda for discussion. And if you want to extend it another year, you've got the majority of the votes, you can extend it in perpetuity if you wish."

With feigned patience, Dad reminded Sonny, "You can bring up a motion for a loan at next year's board meeting."

Sonny insisted, "Well, I understand, but this forces it to the agenda, Sam."

"Well, let me just point out one other thing." Dad continued, "We've been six months trying to get this thing passed and you wouldn't let us bring it to the board…"

Sonny interrupted him, "I can't stop you from doing anything you want…"

"Well, other than you keep on bringing new items up…" Dad added with exasperation.

Mom was also irritated but tried another approach. She asked Sonny, "Well, what do you want?"

Dad attempted to assuage Sonny's dissent, "If for some unforeseen reason, the company has a great year, and is in a great cash flow position, the board would be happy to lend some cash to you."

At the end of this part of the meeting, we agreed that the dividend/loan agreement would expire at the end of January 1990, as Sonny had requested.

When we asked him if he was satisfied with our agreement to his requested change, he said, "You don't have to loan me any money, you have the control, you don't have to loan me any money ever. I can't force you to write me a check."

I asked if there was any further discussion, and Sonny replied, "Well, except to tell you all, it's going to put me in a serious bind. I recognize the posture I'm in, and I can do nothing about it, you know. I'll just have to do the best I can."

The meeting ended and we all left tiredly, forced to have tolerated Sonny's continued provocations. There was a point long ago when we realized that the questioning was done more for the purpose of harassing us than to get real answers. I'm not convinced that Sonny had any desire to get answers. The discussions of that meeting were audio-recorded by both Sonny and the Fultons. To this day, I'm flabbergasted at Sonny's total lack of understanding that Finch existed for other reasons than to make his own life comfortable.

On September 11, 1989, Sonny's attorney, Tom Hudson, sent me a letter again proposing a buyout of Sonny's interest in the company [see Appendix Four]. Hudson tried to play on our sympathies with this letter, but we didn't feel so sympathetic after all of the harassing and degrading conduct Sonny had visited upon all of us. He brought up several methods of buyouts, but still insisted on ridiculously high purchase prices. Hudson started the letter by saying that Sonny was "suffering from the abrupt discontinuance of payments from The Finch Companies." One of the options in the letter was that each party appoint an arbitrator, and that those two appoint a third arbitrator. The other main point of this letter was to divide the assets of the company and for Sonny to lease back his portion to us for operating purposes.

There are a lot of ideas in Hudson's letter which may have appealed to us, had they been offered years ago in a more cordial atmosphere. However, because of the way we felt that Sonny and Hudson had set up such an adversarial relationship, several of these options had been negated. As far as the arbitrator idea, frankly, we weren't sure that his stature as a congressman, and his demonstrated influence with our bankers (and therefore, in our opinion, likely influence with a third arbitrator), might skew the final result of that method. He also mentioned the "abrupt" discontinuance of payments. We had been telling him for years that this needed to be curtailed. I don't hesitate to point out the fact that he received substantially more cash from the company in the five years after I took over as president than he received in the last five years of his administration.

He was personally responsible—not me, and not my family—for changing his lifestyle to a more affluent one. Hudson doesn't even bring up the fact that Sonny was receiving a congressman's salary. In addition, I was getting phone calls from at least one outside business partner demanding that I send money because Sonny owed this person substantial amounts in a self-storage facility venture. As far as the idea of us "splitting the assets" and Sonny leasing his half back to us, again, this would have required a level of trust and camaraderie, which had been destroyed by Sonny's actions at board meetings and with our bankers.

I wrote Hudson and stated that we were not interested in dicing the company into pieces, and that we considered the business to be a single entity. We were still willing to discuss various methods of a financial buyout or financing possibilities.

The letters continued back and forth. On October 13, 1989, Tom Hudson responded with an offer to sell Callahan's stock to us for $2.9 million or he would buy our stock for $3.8 million.

For the previous couple of years, my mother had wanted to begin gifting her stock to Danny and me. This would prevent undue tax liabilities to my mother's future estate. We had thought about getting Ernst & Young to do a valuation of her stock so that we could begin that process. Since Sonny had been so insistent that he be bought out, we felt like now was a good opportunity to get Ernst & Young to evaluate the value of his stock for purchase by the company.

Because there were relatively few comparative situations for the sale of warehousing companies, Ernst & Young relied on multiples from the trucking industry, in large part, for use in their analysis from the market approach. While the results were similar to those reached from the income approach, we were told that the income approach was the more proper way to consider the value of stock in the company.

The report basically resulted in an adjusted value of 100 percent of the operating equity of the Finch Companies to be approximately $2 million. Ernst & Young then applied customary discounts of 20 percent for minority value and another 20 percent discount for lack of marketability of a closely held business. Their conclusion was a fair market value of $626,000 for 48.9 percent of the common stock of the Finch Companies as of October 31, 1989. This seemed to be right in line with our previous calculations, even though we had offered Sonny much more than that.

This was actually a cynical negotiating move by Hudson, especially since we had made it clear that under no circumstances were we willing to sell out to him. Furthermore, we were assured time and time again by our attorneys that the law specifically stated that the majority is not required to purchase the minority's stock, under any circumstances. We had pointed out how ridiculous Hudson's "valuation" of the stock was and we were summarily ignored.

What nobody seemed to grasp is that we had high hopes and aspirations for the future of the company, and we wanted to pursue that direction. In addition, Sonny had so poisoned the atmosphere with his weird attacks at the board meetings and his unwillingness to visit us to see what we were doing, that anything that left him in a position to harass us became an untenable situation.

The numbers they were tossing around were tremendous, and given that the banks had several times told us we were already overextended, those amounts seemed even more unrealistic. In addition, whenever my mother or I would ask Sonny how all of this financing could be accomplished, he would simply tell us that he had some expert in Louisiana who could make it work. All we had to do was agree to the amount and he would work it out. Since we thought the numbers were ridiculous, we could never agree to them.

I still wonder, to this day, what would have happened if we had accepted his offer to buy us out for $3,800,000. We'll never know, since we never had any desire to sell out our future. He knew that very well, which is why it was such a shrewd, cynical tactic.

Hudson asked us to demonstrate any reason we felt his analysis to be wrong. We asked David Park with Ernst & Young to address this in writing. His analysis made several key points for our argument. He reaffirmed our argument that Hudson's original valuation was wrong in substance and violated several tenets of generally accepted accounting procedures, which rendered it useless. Here is one very key part of Park's analysis:

> Regarding the attorney letter, we basically feel the entire analysis is flawed and incorrect. The analysis fails to comply with generally accepted valuation methodology, makes arbitrary assumptions, does not support the basis for the assumptions, confuses the concept of "replacement cost" with "fair market value," and makes several mathematical errors.
>
> The attorney values the company using both a "Capitalized Income Approach" and a "Net Asset Value Approach." We feel both approaches are deficient for a variety of reasons.
>
> The "Capitalized Income Approach" is flawed primarily because the attorney uses the wrong 1987 operating revenues number. The attorney assumes 1987 revenues to be $4,797,603

while the audited financial statements state that total revenues
for the year ending December 31, 1987 were $4,083,265. Using
the attorney's own methodology and assumptions, this $714,338
difference would flow through to the bottom line. Therefore,
"adjusted net operating income", as defined by the attorney,
would be $187,032...not $901,370. Applying the attorney's 10%
capitalization rate, the gross value of the company would be
$1,870,320...not the $9,013,700 stated in the letter. Thus, just
this one wrong assumption caused a $7,143,380 valuation error!

The "Net Asset Value Approach" is also flawed, for a variety
of reasons. In the first place, the valuation of the buildings is on
a "replacement cost new" basis, and is not representative of fair
market value. The attorney's $6,284,385 value might represent
what it would cost to replace the buildings today, but the fact
is that most of the buildings are 10 to 20 years old and worth
nowhere near what it might cost to replace them. The attorney
fails to consider the impact of physical depreciation, as well as
functional and economic obsolescence, and thus greatly over-
states the value of the buildings.

Hudson asked for a rebuttal to his valuation, and I think
David Park does that in spades. We really wanted to find a way
to get this buyout accomplished and put all of this behind us, but
there had to be a realistic starting place. In my response to Sonny
that I wrote on December 20, 1989 [see Appendix Five], I relied
heavily on David Park's letter to explain the fallacy of Hudson's
evaluation [see Appendix Four] of the value of Sonny's stock.

One of the buyout options had to do with spinning off some
of the buildings to Sonny, along with their operations. We looked
into that option, with the understanding that Sonny would lease
the buildings back to us so that we would continue to service our
customers. We were still somewhat leery of this because of the
adversarial nature of the last few years. We had our tax special-
ist, Steve Mixon, investigate some of the ramifications of this
idea. Unfortunately, he came back with research which stated
that both surviving companies would have to have active income,

and not just passive rent/lease income. This would have put us in an untenable situation with our customers.

Sonny kept insisting that there was a way to work the tax problems out, but neither he nor his attorneys ever presented concrete ways to achieve this. I suppose they couldn't understand that by splitting our customers up, which would have been impossible to avoid, we would have had to be in competition. Since he had poisoned the atmosphere, we simply didn't trust what would have eventually happened. For example, Scott Paper would have necessarily been split between us. We had an excellent operating relationship with them and I envisioned future problems with deciding who got what pieces of their business. When Sonny originally opened up the Great Southern Corporation, he put a good piece of Scott's business in that area, to the detriment of Finch Warehousing. I could see that becoming a problem in the future.

The Board of Directors meeting for the 1989 fiscal year was held on February 10, 1990. There were five resolutions presented to the board. First, I was asking for a substantial raise in pay. The salary I was asking for was still substantially below that of comparable positions in our industry and substantially below that which Sonny had been receiving before he left for Washington. The second resolution put my brother on salary-plus-commission structure for the moving division.

The third resolution guarantied full salary to Scott Callahan while he was on leave from the company. He had been unhappy with his duties at the company, so I asked him what he would like to do. He said he had a realtor's license and would like to open up a residential real estate division within the company. We agreed to pursue that, but only after he went out in the real estate market, with another company, and got the training and experience necessary to make that successful. He readily agreed. We would make a final decision on whether to start that venture sometime toward the end of 1990.

The fourth resolution declared a dividend of 50 percent of total 1989 profits to the stockholders. All dividends would continue to be applied to any outstanding balances of the stockholders. The fifth resolution stated that all loans to stockholders or directors would continue to be those made to cover the tax liabilities of the stockholders based on actual quarterly profits. There was much discontent in this meeting from Sonny, but we tolerated it and moved on from there.

We were going through some major challenges with the operations all during the time of these negotiations. As much as we wanted to make something work with Sonny, we needed to spend our energies on the Finch Companies. Our books were showing a profit for 1989 of about $160,000 on revenue of just under $8 million. However, our new trucking division was losing substantial amounts, and we knew we had to make adjustments to make it profitable. We were getting praise for exceptional service from our customers, but it was not translating to the bottom line.

As if we didn't have enough challenges, one of the biggest was about to slap us in the face. At the end of 1989, our books showed a profit of $160,000. I had given bonuses to our employees and officers because I knew they had gone the extra mile during the year. Unfortunately, I had a rude awakening from our outside auditor around late February. Gene Gibbons of Gibbons & Dees had done our yearly audits for years. Over the years, he had been most insistent that Sonny be required to sign a note for the debt he owed the company. Sonny always refused to do that. This time, his news was a total shock. He came to my office and explained to me that our internal books were incorrect in a major way. Instead of making $160,000 profit, we had actually lost approximately $90,000 company-wide.

The retirement of Dan Miller, our longtime, trusted company bookkeeper, had been an important event for the Finch Companies during this time. Dan was one of the most conscientious, trustworthy people I've ever met. Upon hiring a new bookkeeper, Dan trained him, assured me that he was competent, and prepared him for the job. This bookkeeper proved to be totally incompetent. Gene did not believe that the bookkeeper was dishonest or stealing, but just incapable of handling the workload. Ultimately, though, the responsibility for the mistakes of our bookkeeper had to remain mine, as president.

This was an enormous punch in the stomach. I called a meeting of the board and shareholders and explained what had happened. To our staff's credit, especially Louise Cotton, they worked tirelessly, often putting in sixteen- to twenty-hour days to correct the books. It certainly hadn't helped my decision-making as we were growing the company. This by itself would have been a challenge, but it was especially difficult in light of everything else we were going through. Dan Miller returned during this time to help us put the financials back in order. I couldn't thank him enough for his help.

We were in a major cash crunch, which is not a very good way to handle the kind of massive growth we had undertaken. The banks had made it very clear to us that our problems stemmed from three major areas. First, we had declared and paid out more than 97 percent of our profits over the past several years, leaving nothing for regular operations, much less the expansion we were attempting. Second, we had loaned out hundreds of thousands of dollars chiefly to one stockholder, in excess of the earned dividends. Third, of course, the costly expansion into long-haul freight service. It seems crazy now, but we actually thought that we could grow the company fast enough to overcome the first two problems. In order to try to ease the cash crunch, we were attempting to refinance our debt so that we could make our bank payments in a more timely fashion. The confusion from our bookkeeping certainly muddled an already difficult situation.

One of the things I tried to do was keep our bank representatives aware of the things happening at Finch from a business standpoint. Joey Ginn at AmSouth Bank was my main contact, and the person to whom I presented most of my proposals for financing needs. He genuinely seemed to be trying to help, but every decision had to be approved by his superiors. They were very uncomfortable with the losses from the trucking operation, but had also been uncomfortable with our dividend and loan policies in the past. What made it especially difficult was the combination of these. They turned down virtually all of our requests for meaningful refinancing.

With all of the negatives we had, our top people still felt we could turn things around. We had promoted Bruce Byrd to vice president of operations. I felt like I had someone who would work with me and in whom I could trust. We also promoted Marcia Washam to sales and marketing for our warehousing and local trucking operations. She had really grown over the last couple of years and had expressed interest in the sales opening to Bruce. She had been with us for a long time in all of the clerical parts of our business, and had received rave reviews from our customers' accounting and clerical counterparts for her ability to solve any problems they may have had over the years.

We had also hired some other very talented gentlemen—finally, there were people whom I believed could turn us around and approach the potential we felt this venture could attain. In August 1989, we hired Bart Ray, someone with proven qualifications, as the manager for the FDS Division. We also hired Ed Alexander in late 1990, to handle personnel and safety areas for the whole company. Bob Greene became our Controller in August 1990. Jeff Sims and Norman Pierre were our dispatchers for the FDS division. We really felt that we had a team that could turn it around for us. It would take time, though.

Sonny still believed that somehow we could work out some sort of buyout, even with the tough times. He named as his authority on the methodology a man from Baton Rouge, a tax expert, by the name of Ted Jones. At Sonny's request, we sent all of our financials to him. All of his scenarios seemed dependent on spinning off a division of the company. Beginning in September, we knew we had to come to some sort of buyout arrangement. The banks had virtually given up on any meaningful refinancing plan until we could come to an agreement with Sonny. That agreement also had to fit their standards for lending to companies in our predicament. It was quite a catch-22. Sonny wouldn't agree to a plan that would fit the bank's needs, and the bank wouldn't agree to the level of compensation for the Finch Companies' purchase of Sonny's stock.

The negotiating between the Fulton and Callahan families was proceeding dramatically, and with the desperate need for Sonny's cooperation with the banks, we were moving up substantially with our offers. Our offers had grown to approximately $1,600,000 with a possibility of spinning off one of the warehouse divisions. We were very nervous about possible negative consequences to the Fulton side of the deal, but agreed to seriously consider his ideas. In fact, at one point, we were almost ready to make it work, even to the point of sending a letter to Sonny pointing out the circumstances in which we would agree. We left several doors open to leaving the deal during this consideration period because everyone on our side was anxious about the real-life ability to make this work. We were substantially over the amounts for which we had become comfortable.

This was in early October 1990, and we were aware that we would have to obtain a substantial level of cooperation with AmSouth Bank in order to make this work. Even with Sonny's cooperation, I didn't get any good feeling from anyone at the bank that they would go along with anything close to what we needed. We submitted our proposal to AmSouth on October 3, 1990. We were politely rebuffed. Later, Sonny was critical of my going directly to the bank without letting him go to them first; but my family was going to be on the hook for the payments and any consequences, so I felt I needed to know that they were really backing me.

Toward the end of November 1990, I wrote a letter to Sonny in which I proposed an exchange of notes and monthly payments between us. At this point, no financial institution would provide the cash for a buyout, so our offer would be a straight buyout with our own notes. He would also have his substantial debt to the company cancelled. This meant that the offer would be significantly higher than any we had made so far.

For all practical purposes, meaningful negotiations seemed to end after this.

Chapter Eight
Trucking...and Twins!

Still, our biggest challenges involved bringing the overall level of profitability in the Finch Companies back to the level we needed to be successful. Our household goods moving divisions (Allied Van Lines) had been struggling for years, both in Mobile and Montgomery. Since it wasn't really related to the warehousing/trucking businesses we were running, we decided to sell those divisions at the first possible opportunity. We were able to sell the Mobile branch in early April 1991.

We were endeavoring to sell the Montgomery Allied Van Lines branch also, even though it was a different setup. In the late eighties, we were located in a very small, ground-level building located in a rough area of Montgomery. Our secretary had been threatened in her office by local thugs, and ever since that time the doors were kept locked, even during operating hours. It was simply an unacceptable situation. Fred Fields, our manager for the Montgomery operations, was insistent that we look for a better location. We found a great facility at Gunter Industrial Park, which we had hoped would accommodate our moving business as well as allow us to expand our warehousing operations. The 48,000 square-foot building was a substantial improvement over our 11,000 square-foot facility. For a short period, we were able to keep the building full with overflow from Scott Paper in Mobile. After a while though, even that dwindled down and the operations in Montgomery began to be unprofitable. With all of our challenges in Mobile, and the fact that our top staff in Montgomery were close to retiring, it made sense to be looking to concentrate our efforts on the warehousing and trucking divisions.

Our business planning sessions for the 1991 year went very well, and the morale was surprisingly positive as we began the year. We had made several adjustments and had high hopes that they would pay off. Our results for 1990 were mixed, but overall we were profitable. That is not to say that we weren't still in a major cash crunch, because we were. Our profit was only $5,000 on revenue of $7.2 million. This was better than 1989, when we lost about $78,000. We were growing very fast, revenue-wise, but obviously faster than our cash flow was allowing. We were having trouble paying our bank notes in a timely manner and this was surely hampering our ability to negotiate better terms. While it was difficult, the banks were trying to work with us. Unfortunately, most of their remedies called for terms that only made it more challenging in the short run.

All during this period, we were searching for alternatives for financing from other institutions. The word we kept getting was that Sonny had already made it clear to them that it was not a good move to support us at this time. We had expanded our trucking capability through leasing contracts, which had proven to be a very expensive way to do business. While we had started with five tractors and eight trailers in 1988, we were now operating twenty-six tractors and forty-three trailers. Many of our customers told us that with only five units, they would not be able to commit their better freight to us. Scott Paper especially encouraged us to get to a much greater level, and committed more freight to us because of our expansion. In fact, they had culled their freight carriers from more than one hundred different vendors to less than fifteen, and we made the cut.

One of the major difficulties we ran into had to do with the promises made by Ryder. When we began, they assured us that since they had their own insurance arm, our rates would be dramatically lower than if we were to go outside. They also told us that they had a network of cooperative fueling and maintenance facilities throughout the country and their fuel rates were lower than the market averages. Also, they assured us that since they also operated a trucking division, they would gladly cooperate with backhaul opportunities from lower Florida, which was a key route for us. Unfortunately, none of these things turned out to be as helpful as we were told. We had opted for their "full-service" leases, which turned out to be a terrific mistake.

They soon sold off their insurance company and their backhaul services from lower Florida were virtually nonexistent. In addition, our drivers did verify that the fuel prices were lower at their facilities, but those facilities were generally off the beaten path and sometimes hard to find. As we grew, we tried to work out better leasing arrangements for our new trucks. We had some limited success with this, but it would still take years for us to get to the point where we had enough "paid-for" equipment in our fleet.

We did have some good success with attracting and keeping good drivers. We had competitive mileage pay, very good benefits, and our dispatchers made every effort to get our drivers back home in no more than two weeks. That was very important to them. So many had complained that their former employers would make that promise, but more often than not, they could not turn down that next load. Our customers often complimented us on our drivers' professionalism and willingness to work.

We still had a problem with deadhead (empty) miles, but we were attacking them aggressively and having some slow but steady success. However, we were still losing our shirt in the trucking division and we were desperately looking for ways to turn that around. Our warehousing divisions were very success-ful and were receiving some income because of the trucking op-erations, but not enough to offset the trucking losses.

In preparation for our February 1991 board meeting, our management worked diligently to put together a realistic plan of attack using an in-depth analysis of each division with emphasis on strengths, weaknesses, opportunities, and threats (SWOT). We were trying to be realistic about operations and knew that some tough decisions were ahead. We were comfortable with our decision to sell the Mobile moving division, as well as our attempt to sell off the Montgomery moving division. We were still pursuing a buyer for the Montgomery operations, but so far our best prospect was interested in buying the moving operation, but not in occupying the building which we were obligated to lease until 1993. If that were to come to fruition, we would sim-ply do our best to sublease as much of the warehouse as possible until that time.

We came up with a very detailed business plan that we would present at the board meeting, as well as something we wanted to present to banks.

My personal life was also very busy at this time. My wife, Lane, and I were excited that she was pregnant with twins who were due in late April. I had talked her into having a fourth child and we were thrilled when it turned out to be two! I was also still active in several civic groups, including the Jaycees, Kiwanis, and Home of Grace for Women, and had just finished my term as vice chairman of the Alabama Republican Executive Com-mittee. I had decided not to run for reelection because I needed to do everything possible to get the company turned around.

On Saturday, February 2, 1991, I was driving back from a meeting of that committee. When I was about forty miles out-side of Mobile, I got a call from Lane saying that our daughter, Ashley, had fallen down the stairs and hit her head. She was momentarily unconscious, but seemed okay then. Lane decided to take her to the hospital emergency room, just as a precaution. I met them at the hospital, and after a scan, the doctors pronounced our daughter fine.

Sunday morning, Lane awakened me and said that she felt like she was going into labor. It seemed that when Ashley had fallen down the stairs, Lane picked her up and may have strained herself. We rushed to the hospital and were immediately admitted. The situation was very serious. The doctor explained to us that Lane had started labor and if they couldn't stop it quickly, the babies would be born three months premature and would probably not weigh more than a pound or so each. They gave them a 50 percent chance of survival at that point. I don't think we've ever prayed harder. They wanted to transfer Lane to the neonatal emergency center, which was located at another hospital, but the doctor felt like it was too late for that. They would have to administer some medicine to her designed to slow down and stop the contractions. After several hours, the contractions slowed down, then stopped. We were out of danger for the time being.

With our first three children, we did not want to know their sex until they were born. Because of the near tragedy with the twins, we decided to find out so that we could have names for them if something happened. The ultrasound showed two girls. Lane spent a week in the hospital, and then was confined to bed rest at home for seven more weeks. We were able to take advantage of a new drug and new technology for delivering the drug at home. Every three days, I had to stab Lane's leg with a subcutaneous tube which was attached to a metered dispenser, about the size of a pager. Twice daily, we would attach a belt around her belly and then attach a cord from there to the telephone, which then transmitted over the phone to an out-of-town location. After the transmission, someone would call us and tell us how many contractions she had and whether or not to adjust the medication. We were so impressed that we later bought stock in the company, Tokos, and made a healthy return!

One of our best memories during that time was the celebration of our tenth wedding anniversary. My brother, Danny, and his wife, Angela, lived across the street from us and were invaluable in helping us through this difficulty. On our anniversary they came over, decorated our den, and cooked a delicious steak dinner for us. During her bed rest, Lane was allowed to come downstairs once per day and sit on the couch in the den. That day, she came downstairs and a table was set with fancy china and flowers just for us. They took the kids with them, allowing us to be alone to celebrate. We had just begun eating when Lane felt some contractions and had to go lie down on the couch. Nevertheless, it was still a memorable evening and we were very grateful to Danny and Angela.

On February 4, 1991, we held our annual board meeting for the company. After all of the consternation we had been through with so many of the other meetings, I tried to be as prepared as possible. We had only preliminary figures for the year's profit-loss, and there were always some adjustments made by the auditors which we didn't have yet. However, we felt comfortable that, overall, we had achieved a profit, however slight. At this meeting, we had estimated the final profit to be $78,000, but in actuality it was $5,101 for the year.

Regardless, our cash flow position was very weak, so we voted to declare no dividends, nor allow any loans to shareholders. We also voted to do away with Sonny's $1,000 monthly director's fee, since he was the only one receiving that pay. Sonny was doing everything he could to harass us, and while that was very unhelpful, we certainly didn't feel he should receive special benefits and pay to do that.

Sonny argued that he was going to have to pay his own taxes, and that we should at least agree to advance him an amount to cover those. Our side of the family was also responsible for our own taxes, so we weren't being unfair to him. As a matter of fact, when we thought we had a profit the last year, we did forward tax money to him for his estimated tax payment. When it turned out that we had really experienced a loss, my mother, who was in a similar tax situation, received about $50,000 in tax refunds because of the overpayment. Sonny received about the same amount, and when we asked him to return it to the company, he refused. We just figured he could take that refund and pay this year's liability.

We had been beaten up so badly by Sonny that we weren't going to give any extra benefits to him that we weren't giving to ourselves. The irony of this situation is that even though the eventual audit showed that we only made $5,101, the shareholders were responsible for more income because of our cash shortfall. By then, Sonny owed the company more than $400,000, and the company owed my mother more than $300,000. Sonny's account was growing even without further loans because he had insisted years ago that his negative account be charged interest and any positive accounts earn interest at prime rate. However, at the end of the year, we didn't have the cash to pay the interest owed to my mother, so that amount could not be expensed, and therefore increased the tax liability. The irony is that if Sonny hadn't taken so much cash out of the company, we could have paid Mom and lowered both Sonny and Mom's liability. Additionally, Sonny didn't pay any of the interest on his account, but we were required to show that as income to the company. (Later, we would be criticized as though we somehow did this intentionally to him.)

We also approved a motion during the board meeting to proceed with the sale of our moving divisions. At this point, Scott Callahan made a motion to open a real estate company called Homefinders. It was to be an agency that catered specifically to buyers, as their agents, rather than representing the sellers as was customary. During the more than fourteen months Scott had been selling for Marie McConnell Realty, he had only closed on two sales. Furthermore, he did not take advantage of the training that Marie offered and we really didn't feel he had done the work needed to make his real estate venture successful. Sonny and Scott were furious.

Around this period of time, I received a phone call from one of Sonny's good friends, Monty Collins. Monty was a vice president at one of the local banks and served as a paid associate in Sonny's congressional office. I had always gotten along well with Monty in the past and I distinctly remember a conversation with him on the phone once in which he commiserated with me that Sonny would do anything in the world for a stranger, but somehow found ways to hurt those closest to him.

During this phone call though, Monty sounded almost desperate. His call came seemingly out of the blue, and he immediately started telling me that we had to get out of the trucking business—now! I explained to him that if I had a way to get out of the leases on the trucks and trailers, I would be happy to get out of it. I explained that we had studied the cost of getting out, and under the best of circumstances, it would cost us more than $700,000. Originally, we had estimated the get-out cost at just over $300,000. This analysis was done incorrectly by our controller, whom we had fired for incompetence. We had explained all of this to Sonny after he demanded that we "divorce" ourselves from the trucking business, as though our contracts could just be ignored. I further explained to Monty that our leases would begin ending the next year and we would be in a better position to make a profit or dramatically decrease our exposure, but we couldn't do it under the current situation.

We did start negotiations with Ryder to remove some of the more cumbersome details in their leasing contract; things we felt were making it almost impossible to succeed. We did broach the subject of getting out of the contracts, but they were adamant that for us to get out, we had to raise the money to buy out the remainder of the contract. They were not very accommodating,

I guess because they didn't feel that they had to compromise much. We were running late on payments, but we always paid.

The pressure was becoming intense. Our ability to pay the bank notes and other obligations was very challenging. I stayed in constant touch with all of our vendors and, I guess, because many companies were having difficulty, especially the trucking industry, as long as we kept in touch they seemed willing to work with us. We had some really anxious moments with the banks, but I understood their position. They would not renegotiate our loans until we could establish a steady on-time record of payment. We had so much short-term debt that we had difficulty catching up. In addition, many of our customers were taking their time paying us.

Believe it or not though, I really felt like we had a handle on everything and we did not have a single vendor tell us that they refused to do business with us. We just needed to keep things together until we could work our way out of the truck leases, which would begin in a substantial way in 1992 and 1993. Of course, this meant there was no way we were in a position to consider buying out Sonny. I had come to realize also that we needed to maintain a positive view to the outside world. Sonny was making it known, as I was learning from several people, that we were ruining the company; his announcements had the potential of accelerating that possibility. But as long as our service level remained high, our customers would stick with us, and they did.

The progress on the home front was promising…the twins were growing in the womb, and all signs pointed to healthy little girls. Our doctor told us that many times they don't let twins go to full-term, and our date would be April 1, 1991, about one month early. We were really getting excited! We hadn't told anyone else that we were having girls, nor did we tell anyone their names. On Monday, April Fools' Day, we went to the hospital and got ready. They had told us to stop the labor-inhibiting medication the night before because they expected quick response. We walked a few laps around the halls in the hospital until Lane felt that it was imminent. That day our twin girls, Kathryn Fisher and Kary Abell, were born. They weighed five pounds, fourteen ounces and six pounds, one ounce, respectively...very, very healthy. I can't tell you how much of a miracle their healthy birth seemed to us!

I vividly remember my mother calling to let Sonny's wife, Karen, know that things had turned out well. It was painfully obvious that Sonny had answered the phone and then just handed it over to Karen.

Thomas William Finch

Tom and Genevieve Finch

This is Tom Finch at their beach house in Gulf Shores. Years later, Hurricane Frederick would completely destroy this wonderful family getaway.

From left to right: (unknown), Jack Fulton, S. C. Fulton, Betty Jo Fulton, Geraldine Finch, and Sonny Callahan at my parents' wedding reception.

Grandpa Finch giving me advice on becoming a warehousing magnate.

Betty Jo Fulton, Karen Callahan, Sonny, and S. C. Fulton at Sonny and Karen's wedding.

The reception…happier times for the two families.

Me, Karen, Sonny, Patrick, Scott, and Danny reading the returns from Sonny's first election.

Dad and Mom introduced to Governor George Wallace by Sonny.

Sonny was the speaker when I received my Eagle award.

My brother and I representing our company at a career fair.

Clockwise, seated, from upper left, Genevieve Finch, Mom, Dad, Sonny, and Karen. Standing, on right, Daniel and Danny Fulton. We were celebrating someone's birthday.

This was my desk when I began my unexpected career at Marie McConnell Realty. My desktop shrank to about one tenth of my area at Finch. Took some adjustment…

Chapter Nine
The Lawsuit

Things were rocking along, with continuing challenges on the cash flow front, but nothing that we weren't handling.

I was sitting in my office when Bruce Byrd called me and in a strange voice, asked, "Have you seen the paper this morning?"

I replied with a chuckle, "No, why, have I been arrested?"

"Not really…Sonny is suing y'all."

He brought the article to me and there it was in the April 25, 1991 issue of the Mobile Press Register.

Mobile Press Register   **April 25, 1991**

Callahan sues over business

U.S. Rep. Sonny Callahan R-Ala. has filed a lawsuit in connection with a controversy surrounding the sale of his interest in a local business.

The lawsuit filed in Mobile County Circuit Court claims that Callahan, who owns 48.9 percent of the stock in Finch Companies, Inc., is embroiled in a controversy over Callahan's sale of his interest to the other owners.

Defendants named in the suit include Thomas W. Fulton, Elizabeth J. Fulton, Daniel R. Fulton, Samuel C. Fulton and The Finch Companies.

The suit claims that on July 7, 1988, "after receiving a proposal from plaintiff (Callahan) for the sale of his interest in the Finch Companies, Inc., the individual Fulton defendants did offer to purchase plaintiff's interest at a figure that was much less than the fair market value of plaintiff's interest in the corporation and less than a third of plaintiff's offer."

It also alleges the defendants "caused a reduction in the dividends credited to plaintiff and retained up to 50 percent of the net profits earned in 1988, and distributed none of the profits earned in 1990."

Callahan alleges in the lawsuit "that the defendants' retention of the net profits of The Finch Companies, Inc. was without justification and for the express purpose of forcing plaintiff to accept defendants' unreasonably low offer to purchase."

The suit adds: "As a consequence of the aforesaid actions, plaintiff has had to pay taxes on his share of the entire net profits of The Finch Companies, Inc. and yet has only received fifty percent of that share in 1988 and nothing in 1990."

I immediately called Watson Smith, our attorney, and told him what was in the paper. He asked me if we had been served any papers, because that is what normally happens before something like that got into the paper. We had received nothing; in fact, we weren't served until late that afternoon.

Ironically, another article in the same edition of the Mobile Press Register featured a picture of a new, 63-foot, custom-built houseboat Sonny had purchased to live on and to be moored in Washington, DC.

Mobile Press Register   **April 25, 1991**

AP photo

Home on the river

This 63-foot, custom-built houseboat anchored at the Gangplank Marina on the Potomac River in Washington, D.C., is the home of Rep. Sonny Callahan, R-Ala. The boat, built from scratch by Steiner Shipyard, owned by Russell Steiner, at Bayou La Batre, Ala., is his Washington home necessitated by high rent in the nation's capital, according to Callahan. The boat is named the Kelly C. after the Callahan's 15-year-old daughter.

We were incredulous. We didn't believe that his charges stood a prayer of succeeding. First, we had been assured that, by Alabama law, and I suppose the law in most states, the majority shareholders were not required to purchase the minority's shares under any circumstances. We were told that the value of anything for sale was the agreement of terms by a willing seller and a willing buyer. Since we had tried to come to agreement but couldn't agree, we were not willing buyers, nor were we willing sellers.

Second, the allegation in the article that we had caused a reduction in the dividends was true, but, as far as I could tell, not an unwise business decision. It's also misleading, because the net effect of the 1988 dividend declaration was approximately 75 percent of the profits. The 1990 profit was only $5,101. Further, there was no mention that we had forwarded more than $50,000 in loans for tax payments in 1989, which the government had refunded to him after we discovered that the shareholders wrote off losses instead of anticipated profits. While my mother had returned that money to company, Sonny kept his refund even though he owed substantially more than that to Finch.

For the reasons mentioned above, Sonny had been given more than enough cash to cover his tax liabilities from Finch operations. Frankly, we weren't trying to force Sonny to sell to us at any price. We had simply decided our efforts needed to be focused on bringing the company back to a fiscally sound position. I had even assured Sonny that I would do everything I could in the future to try to bring the value of his stock up to what he wanted, but that it would take years. He said he couldn't wait that long and that I was running the company into the ground anyway.

Not surprisingly, the lawsuit caused a major furor among all of our employees, customers, and vendors. I spent the next couple of weeks meeting with all of them, especially our major customers and the bankers. I was especially concerned with Scott Paper Company, with whom the vast majority of our business was committed. They were aware of the friction between Sonny and us, but not the extent—heck, I wasn't even aware of the extent.

As far as Sonny's timing of the suit, I really believe that his intention was to do it sooner; but I'm sure that he must have delayed it until our twins were born and healthy. I'm still thankful for that, if that is what he was doing. Danny and Angela had recently given us their good news: they were expecting a baby in November. Oh well, I guess Sonny wouldn't wait that much longer.

Tom Hudson, Sonny's attorney, sent us a series of interrogatory questions. We were given thirty days to answer his interrogatories; and in the meantime, Watson Smith introduced us to Brock Gordon, one of the partners of the firm of Johnstone,

Adams, Bailey, Gordon, and Harris. Brock was to represent us in the actual litigation proceedings.

Anyone who has been through this kind of ordeal understands how tedious and frustrating the "discovery" process becomes. The same questions are asked in several different ways, ostensibly to trip you up. We answered them and submitted some of our own to Sonny. Outside of that, we tried to maintain as normal a life as possible.

With five kids, involvement in several civic activities, and trying to do everything possible to turn the trucking situation around, the lawsuit just became another thing to add to my list. Because I was locally active and Sonny was so politically well known, we couldn't go anywhere without the lawsuit becoming a topic of conversation. Frankly, a lot of people who had known the families for decades were shocked and not a little angry about this; after all the years in which the Fulton family had supported Sonny in all of his endeavors, political and personal, those who knew both families could not believe he would do this.

One of the things that struck me was the number of people who had been present years ago at the Mobile County Republican Executive Committee meeting, in which I had staunchly defended and promoted Sonny. They said they could not believe this was being done after all of that.

I was a member of the Mobile Kiwanis Club, one of the oldest in the country. So many of those members had known Sonny for years and knew how close the families had been. They just shook their heads, and for the most part seemed to support us. After a few weeks, though, the lawsuit just faded into the background.

We were continuing to have problems in the trucking area, but we still felt like we would work our way through it. Our employees were great…they knew how hard everyone was working to turn things around. Our warehousing divisions were doing great; the furniture leasing division, under my mother's leadership, was having record profits. We had sold the Mobile moving division, and had leads on selling the Montgomery branch. For the first time, I really felt like we had the right personnel in place. However, as optimistic as I tended to be, even I thought it was going to be awhile before we could get the trucking division profitable.

I continued trying to find a way to get out from under the leases, and in some cases, was able to refinance some equipment under better leases, but it was obvious that we wouldn't be able to completely solve that problem until the leases started ending in 1992. We had also done everything we could to attack the cash flow problem. We had more than enough accounts receivable out there to cover our obligations...we just weren't collecting fast enough. Unfortunately, I had been forced to use a factoring company with ridiculous terms. I really didn't have many other choices.

We were given the opportunity to rent a building in Hattiesburg, Mississippi for a Scott Paper–related account that involved trucking and warehousing. It was a great opportunity and led to a very amusing situation. Bruce and I scheduled a meeting with the mayor and some council members to sign the lease for the building. We were surprised that there was going to be a press conference. Apparently, that building was part of a city industrial project, and had formerly been a K-Mart or some such storefront. When we showed up, we had to somehow make it sound like a bigger deal than it was, because we were only going to hire one or two locals, at the most, while sending one of our guys from Mobile. There were news people, cameras, and other dignitaries there. The elected officials kept telling the media that if things went well, we would be expanding our operations and hiring more people. I suppose that was possible. The other thing about that trip was that as tight as things were, we were pushing the limits on everything—including running out of gas and coasting into a gas station bone dry.

To make matters even more interesting, we were in the middle of union contract negotiations. Many of our employees had expressed an interest in getting rid of the union. Our wages and benefits had increased over the years and we had demonstrated how important our employees were to us. The interesting thing to me was that even though the steward had tried to recruit the long-haul drivers into the bargaining unit, those drivers were adamantly opposed to joining. Rather than fighting that battle, the union stuck with the warehousing and moving workers as their membership. They set up a vote, but kept making it difficult for those members of the bargaining unit to find out about the vote. As it turned out, they won the vote on continuing the union representation by a razor-thin margin. However, many of the employees who were against it were confused about the voting date and time, and more than one told me that when they showed up to vote, they were told it was too late.

We went ahead and negotiated a good contract that included virtually everything that we were asked (after the perfunctory posturing period). The only thing we would not agree to was the check-off provision. This is the requirement that company was required to deduct union dues from the members' paychecks. The vote on the contract was held off-premises on a Sunday morning at a local church. I was told it passed on a 2-1 vote. I don't mean that was the ratio…it was two guys voting yes and one guy voting no.

Shortly thereafter, I received this letter from the union that many of my friends in the warehousing and trucking business found very unusual and amusing:

Dear Sir,

Due to no interest on the part of the employees, this is to advise you that Teamsters Local Union NO. 991 has no further interest in being the collective bargaining representative for employees of Finch Company, Inc., under Certification #15-RD-679.

Therefore, this date, we relinquish our rights as the exclusive bargaining representative.

We had really been upset with Tom Hudson's involvement in this lawsuit. He had represented the Finch Companies, and in doing so had been privy to all kinds of inside information about us. It still galls me that even though Tom Hudson worked with the company, and while I was always very open with him in the past, he ended up having prepared the way for this lawsuit. We weren't really very secretive people, so we felt as though we had opened ourselves up to him in the past. In fact, at one point in the price negotiations for Sonny's stock, I was so naïve that I mentioned to Dan Miller that I thought Tom was doing everything he could to help us work this thing out, and that I was sure he would be reasonable. In fact, I just assumed Sonny's negotiating tactics that I had witnessed in labor negotiations inspired his first offer. He had always said to come in high at first, and then let things settle down into a reasonable position.

Dan Miller had attended at least one of the meetings between Sonny and Tom, or at least had been privy to some of their intentions. When I told Dan that I thought Tom would be reasonable and would keep family harmony in mind, he pulled me aside and explained to me that it wasn't going that way at all. He stated very clearly that Hudson was no friend of ours and was operating in a very adversarial way, much more combative than we knew. It was with that in mind that we ultimately discontinued the agreement to fund Hudson with a letter dated August 9, 1988.

Our original letter to Hudson only authorized him to represent Sonny in price negotiations. When we started going through discovery later, we found this letter dated December 3, 1987, from Hudson to Sonny:

Dear Sonny:

You asked that I advise you of the rights of a minority shareholder. The more important statutory rights granted to minority shareholders in Alabama are as follows:

1. A minority shareholder has the right to vote his shares on all matters coming before the shareholders of the corporation (i.e., the election of directors). If the articles of incorporation adopt cumulative voting, a 49% shareholder would be assured of the ability to elect a certain number of directors (1 out of 3; 3 out of 5; 3 out of 7, etc.) See Code Section 10-2A-53.

2. A minority shareholder holding at least 5% of the stock of a corporation can examine the books and records of the corporation in person, or by agent or proxy, at any reasonable time or times, etc. Any corporate officer or manager who fails to allow inspection without reasonable cause is subject to a penalty equal to 10% of the value of the shares owned by such shareholder. This could be substantial. See Section10-2A-79.

3. Each shareholder, including minority shareholders, has the right to receive (within 120 days after the close of a corporation's fiscal year) a financial statement, including balance sheet, for the corporation's immediately preceding fiscal year. The financial statement must be prepared in accordance with generally accepted accounting principles. General accepted accounting principles rules are highly technical and are easily breached. If a minority shareholder were of a mind to "nitpick", this could be one fertile area for examination.

4. A 49% minority shareholder can block any merger or consolidation in which the corporation is a participant (See Section 10-2A-142); can block any sale of all or substantially all assets of the corporation other than in the ordinary course of business (Section 10-2A-161); and can block any voluntary dissolution of the corporation (Section 10-2A-181 and Section 10-2A-182).

5. All shareholders (majority and minority) have a right to be free from insider manipulation of the value of corporate stock or bonds with an eye toward purchase of such stock or bonds at an artificially depressed price (see Section 10-2A-71).

6. Under Code Section 10-2A-195, a minority shareholder may bring an action to involuntarily dissolve a corporation where:

   (a) a deadlock exists among the directors of the corporation and the shareholders are unable to break such deadlock and the situation will result in irreparable injury to the corporation.

(b) those in control are participating in illegal, oppressive or fraudulent acts; or

(c) assets of the corporation are being wasted or misapplied; or

(d) the shareholders of the corporation are deadlocked and have been unable, for a period including two successive annual meetings, to elect directors of the corporation to succeed those whose terms have expired.

(e) the corporation is insolvent.

7. A minority shareholder may bring a shareholder's derivative action in the name of the corporation in any instance where those in control will not cause the corporation to exercise its legal rights; for example, where the majority or a member of the majority is misappropriating corporate assets and will not allow the corporation to exercise its legal rights against him.

In addition to the statutorily provided rights, minority shareholders are entitled to certain other rights such as the right to participate, pro rata, in any distribution made by a corporation with respect to its stock (i.e., dividends). These other rights amount to a fiduciary duty on the part of the majority to act fairly and with full disclosure in dealing with the minority shareholders. Minority shareholders have used this duty of fair dealing to force the majority to pay dividends, to stop "insider" deals between the corporation and members of the majority, and to otherwise prevent the majority from discriminating against or trying to "freeze out" the minority.

Clearly, a minority shareholder who vigorously pursues his legal rights can cause a variety of problems for management by protesting everything from how certain items of depreciation are treated on financial statements, to questioning the reasonableness of compensation paid to majority officers and directors. There are not many cases in Alabama dealing with minority shareholders rights, however, in other areas of the country there is a growing volume of case law concerning these rights. Basically, the idea seems to be that the majority must deal equitably and fairly with the minority in all respects and the minority is entitled to keep a watchful eye on the majority to insure that the majority honors that obligation.

We are exploring various methods for the sale of your interests in the company in order to find the one which may have the
most tax advantage. As we begin to develop these alternatives,
would you like for us to discuss them with Jean [*sic*] Gibbons?

Best regards,
Victor T. Hudson
For the firm

This letter is very important for many reasons. First, the
Finch Companies paid Tom Hudson to give Sonny his advice
on how to sue us. That was never part of the agreement—our
agreement was for price negotiations. I can't overstate this aspect.
After we found out about this letter, a whole battery of unusual
and bizarre behavior by Sonny became clear.

The board meeting we held in January 1989, the one that was
not concluded until May, now became clear. Now we understood Sonny's motivation for dissecting every item on the statements. What was almost comical and seemed so bizarre then
was that we had not changed the methods of depreciation at all
from those we had used when Sonny was presiding. He just kept
asking, "If the depreciation expense in Branch 2 was x in April,
and y in May, what will it be next year and at the end of this
year?" We were so puzzled because we couldn't figure out what
he was trying to find out; therefore, we couldn't exactly answer
in any way that seemed to satisfy him.

As far as compensation, Sonny seemed most interested in
what I was being paid. Never mind that for the first three or four
years of my administration we had record profits and grossed
more than twice the revenue of any of his years. I was still paid
substantially less than he was. Additionally, he actually made
more in compensation in the first five years of my administration
from Finch alone, compared to his compensation in the last five
years of his administration of all the individual companies to-

gether. I had been very careful to get comparable and defensible information from industry sources.

As far as the ability to see the financials of the company, we supplied him with monthly profit-loss statements and monthly balance sheets. When he was president, we didn't even keep monthly balance sheets. Furthermore, our company auditor was also his personal accountant. We never withheld any financial documents from anyone. His son Scott even worked in our office for most of those years and had full access to every document. We wondered why, out of the blue, Sonny started complaining that he wasn't receiving the monthly statements. We were sending them the same way we always had, but now, somehow, he wasn't receiving them. Therefore, I started hand delivering them to his house, and when he told me that wasn't necessary, I had them mailed, certified with return-receipt requested.

When Sonny started recording the board meetings, we started recording them also. He kept complaining that he couldn't find out what was going on at the company. We have tapes of everyone in my family pleading with him to come out to the company at his convenience and we would be thrilled to show him anything and everything he had questions about. He refused to do that.

There were plenty of other examples. Once, during negotiations, Sonny invited me to sit out on his dock on Dog River. We were to discuss the conditions under which he would help us influence the bank to help with the debt refinancing we so desperately needed. One of his requirements was that we give him 50 percent control over any decisions we made. This would give him complete veto power, but more than that, it would give him the ability to create the "deadlock" Hudson had described in his letter. Now it was apparent that Sonny was trying to set up the premises for minority shareholder lawsuits provided by Hudson.

It's very interesting that the lawsuit which Sonny filed in 1991 came word for word from paragraph six in that letter. That letter was sent to Sonny in December of 1987 and it took more than three years of pulling individual actions, out of context, to put together this lawsuit. There was more effort put into fashioning a lawsuit than there was in coming to the company and holding meaningful discussions about what we were doing and how to facilitate meaningful ways of succeeding. That's sad.

Both our attorneys and our family felt that Tom Hudson's manipulations in this matter were unfair and unethical. Something needed to be done about Hudson. All of our side felt that he was more of an impediment to getting a fair deal out of our negotiations, and if he were not involved, maybe Sonny would get an attorney interested in solving the impasse, rather than destroying a family business in pursuit of a victory for his client. Our attorneys filed a petition to have Hudson removed because of a conflict of interest.

There were going to be some appearances before the judge who had been assigned to our case. Judge Braxton Kittrell was the chief judge at the time and appointed himself to this case. Brock and Watson were to have some preliminary appearances before Judge Kittrell in late July.

The next week, we went to court to have Hudson removed. Bobo (pronounced Bob-Oh) Cunningham, one of the better-known attorneys in town, represented Tom Hudson, but even he couldn't protect Hudson from himself. In one of the funniest things I've ever seen in a courtroom, Tom Hudson took the stand and immediately denied ever having represented the Finch Companies as their corporate lawyer, adding that he had only been involved peripherally in any of our business affairs.

Brock Gordon handed Hudson a letter my brother had found in our office and asked Tom to read it to the court. Hudson looked at it, stammered, and started making excuses as to the content.

Brock looked at the judge and said, "Your honor, I'm simply asking Mr. Hudson to read the letter he wrote to Tommy Fulton."

Kittrell ordered Hudson to read the letter. "Dear Tommy, As your corporate attorney,..." he began.

Kittrell let his gavel fall immediately and ordered the attorneys from both sides to meet him in his chambers. Even Hudson started toward the chambers until Kittrell assured him that his presence there was not required.

After some discussion, Brock and Watson sat down with us and explained that Hudson's side had agreed to withdraw from the case immediately in return for our holding him harmless from possible action against him. Dad and Danny did not want to relieve Hudson from future action, but they gave in to my mother and me in our desire to put Hudson's involvement behind us. Today, that seems like a mistake since what Hudson did was a huge ethical violation, and we probably would have been able to recover handsomely from his actions.

The circumstances surrounding our business at that time motivated us to drop Hudson and just move on. We increasingly had to assure our customers and vendors that everything was going to work out just fine, and that all of this would be behind us soon. Not releasing Hudson just seemed to be an impediment to getting this nightmare to end. We also thought that, surely, if Sonny got competent counsel, we could reasonably expect negotiations to be carried out on a civil basis...Boy, were we ever mistaken!

With Hudson removed, we expected Bobo Cunningham to become Sonny's new attorney; but they apparently weren't interested for reasons that would not be made clear to us. Sonny turned to Hand, Arendall, Bedsole, Greaves, & Johnston, who had hired former Congressman Jack Edwards as one of their attorneys. Jerry McDowell signed on as Sonny's attorney with assistance from David Quittmeyer. Jerry, who reminded me of the sort of "old-timey" Southern lawyer, had just been named president of the Mobile Bar Association. Quittmeyer brought visions of Poindexter nerdishness to mind, with the bowtie and all. There would now be some delay time so that the new attorneys could familiarize themselves with the case.

We continued putting out fires at the company and tried to keep morale as positive as possible. Our negotiations with Ryder were ongoing and I really felt like their manager, Ken Buurma, was trying hard to work with us. It just seemed like any progress was enormously slow. In the meantime, we weren't getting the profit situation in the trucking division turned around anywhere near as fast as we needed. Our other divisions were doing fine, but the small victories we were achieving in trucking were operational efficiencies which would pay off eventually, but not in the short run. We had improved our empty miles percentage and even our downtime for maintenance, but all of this was going to take more time.

One of the funnest things we did was our "ice-cream social," which had been started by Louise Cotton, one of our longest and most trusted accounting staffers. On those hot August afternoons, it was a blessed relief to sample every kind of homemade ice cream you could imagine. More importantly, it just set up good face time with all of our people at the company and assured them that we were going to come out of these challenges in good shape. I can't tell you how much it meant to my family to receive their support!

I was pleased with the professionalism we had from the staff who were on board at this time. We had hired proven staff for all levels of the trucking division, from managers to dispatchers to regulatory experts. In our accounting department, the office clerical staff was very effective and was headed up by our controller, Liz Forbis, who seemed very attentive to detail. The only thing we didn't have was time.

In late September, we proceeded with the depositions with the attorneys. Depositions are such a strange process, in which the goal seems to be to ask the same questions in several different ways to see if you would come up with something different from what you had already answered in the interrogatories. Then, those answers will be picked to pieces and used in whatever un-related context that allows the other side to make you to come across as a liar or an idiot. The uninitiated among us would have thought the purpose of all of this questioning would be to find the truth. In reality, I learned that the purpose really is to find any nugget that can be twisted and turned into total rubbish.

It didn't seem to matter what your answers were—the succeeding questions ignored that. I sat through Sonny's deposition and I felt like I was listening either to a Martian or a zombie. The answers to some of the questions were so foreign to the truth that I couldn't believe this whole thing was real. I didn't mind my deposition, and somehow really thought that I could explain everything we were trying to do, both with the company and with Sonny and the buyout negotiations…but that's not at all the purpose of these things.

We wrapped up the questioning in the period of about a week, and the date for the trial was set for Tuesday, October 15, 1991. We were about to see one of the most amazing and mind-blowing exhibitions in our lives.

Chapter Ten
Courtroom Chaos

I was kind of excited about getting to trial and getting this thing over and behind us. I knew that we were right and just figured that everyone else would see this once we were able to explain it to them. We had specifically asked for a jury trial because we thought your average citizen would understand that we were not interested in harassing or oppressing Sonny, or anything else like that.

This was also around the same time that the banking scandal had been exposed in Congress, in which a lot of members had been caught writing bad checks. The "bank" for Congress covered those checks and there was much criticism of congressmen for their personal fiscal habits. We felt that Sonny had done that to us by building up such a huge negative account with Finch. We thought the jury would see that.

We were also made aware of Judge Kittrell's reputation as a very "political" judge. While Sonny was now a Republican, he had been a Democrat, as was Kittrell, for most of his life.

There had been several newspaper articles during the summer, written by Renee Busby of the Mobile Press Register, which addressed the attempts to settle this thing out of court. Garry

Mitchell, from the Montgomery Advertiser, was also covering the proceedings. Trying to go through this in a quiet, discreet way was impossible.

At the beginning of a trial, the lawyers go through all kinds of discussion with the judge on what would and would not be allowed for discussion during the trial. Brock, along with Alan Christian, who was brought on board a few weeks prior to trial, wanted to introduce something called the "clean hands" defense. Their reasoning went back to some of the maneuvers Sonny had used back when he was president of Finch Warehousing and had started his competing entity, Great Southern Corporation, which serviced portions of accounts that we already had at Finch. His exact manipulations for recombining Great Southern back into the Finch Companies were rather complicated; but we felt that the essentials of this needed to be exposed to the jury. The judge ended up disallowing that line of questioning because he felt that we had lived with it this long and if we didn't like it, we should have done something about it back then. The plain fact of the matter is that we only truly discovered a great deal of the details of what happened as we were preparing for the trial.

Jerry McDowell gave the opening statements for Sonny and I have to admit I found it interesting, until I realized he was talking about us and some evil scheme to attack this poor, defenseless congressman. He went through all of those allegations listed in Tom Hudson's letter, which described to Sonny how to set up the lawsuit in the first place. He also started the idea that we were trying so fervently to buy Sonny out. There were so many misleading and blatantly false statements that I was having a hard time sitting still. I wanted to argue right then.

After McDowell finished, it was time for Brock Gordon to make our opening statement. As you can imagine, I thought it was powerful and truthful. We showed that, while I had made some business errors, I also had some tremendous successes; and, whatever my faults, I was not dishonest or unethical. Brock also tried to explain that we had supported Sonny in so many different ways over the years, including allowing him to borrow in excess of $400,000 more than the company owed him. Since Sonny had decided to ignore that effort, we felt that he should pay that back, which would, in turn, solve most of our financial challenges.

After McDowell was given a short period to rebut Brock, I was called to the stand. Let me state right here…I am very poorly suited for this method of conversation, which requires the ability to stop your answers whenever possible with yes or no. It's that old tome you hear about courtroom questioning, "Tell me, yes or no, have you stopped beating your wife?"—there is no yes or no. I'm not sure I would be able to do that, even today. So many of McDowell's questions were of that persuasion.

It didn't take long for McDowell to get me into the "long-answers mode" of testifying. He began quickly taking what I considered to be demeaning cheap shots. He made constant assertions that the only reason anyone in the Fulton family received anything from Finch was that "we were family." He took shots at me, my parents, my brother, and anyone else on our side. Several times, he referred to my father as "your daddy" in a condescending tone. I guess that's considered good "lawyering," but I found it very annoying.

The other thing he did was constantly separate any of the profitable divisions of the company from the unprofitable ones, with the assertion that the good ones ran themselves and the bad ones were all my fault. I didn't mind taking blame for the unprofitable ones, as long as it was viewed in perspective.

Another tactic he used was to infer constantly that our family was diligently trying to buy Sonny out of the company. In response to one of those questions, I launched into an impassioned explanation that Sonny came to us to be bought out, insisting that he was unhappy with the direction of the company. That was in late 1987, before the trucking division, and during the most profitable years ever. What was evident was that we had begun letting Sonny know that we were not going to be able to let him continue to drain the cash assets of the company in the manner that he had been. In addition, and in all fairness to Sonny, it only makes sense to want to get out of something in which you are no longer interested. I fully understand and appreciate that.

Then came the first plea from McDowell to the judge that I not be allowed to give a speech. Brock told the judge that I was being responsive, McDowell said I wasn't.

Judge Kittrell said, "I don't think what he is getting ready to say is a response. You have a right to explain your answer." Well, that was confusing!

Again, McDowell asked me a question in which he tried to tie my parents' intention to begin gifting their stock to Danny and me, with an attempt to buy out Sonny's shares. This was a key component of their case against us. However, it had nothing to do with our assigning a target for his shares. When Sonny asked us to buy him out, we first looked into the possibility of the corporation buying his stock in addition to our buying it individually. Obviously, my parents didn't need any more shares. That would have made it even more difficult to pass their shares down to us. What McDowell was attempting to infer was that somehow we were attempting to intentionally lower our estimation of the value of shares so we could minimize the impact on my parents' estate.

On the surface, I could see how it may have appeared that way. The problem was that the truth was otherwise. I tried to make clear to everyone that Sonny insisted we buy him out, and after studying the options, the only viable method would have been for Danny and me to purchase his shares. After admonishing me to "answer the question," the judge did allow me to expand on the truth that we didn't have a personal preference regarding the buyout and that since Sonny insisted on being bought out, we were open to any viable method.

We broke for lunch with our attorneys and discussed how we felt things were going so far. I felt comfortable that I was going to be able to get the truth out, but I hated the way it was getting piecemealed.

After lunch, McDowell launched into the process of our starting the trucking division. He brought up the point that, while it was approved unanimously, Sonny was not particularly in favor of it. He also brought up the fact that I had projected a profit for that division in 1988, and that Sonny had asked if there was any way it would lose more than $50,000 that year. I had told Sonny that, no, I didn't feel that we would lose more than that.

Later that afternoon, McDowell asked me about the fact that we were starting the trucking division at about the same time we were beginning negotiations to buy Sonny out of the company. Again, I tried to stress to the court that the one had nothing to do with the other.

McDowell then went back to questioning my 1988 projections for the trucking division, and he said that I promised we would not lose more than $50,000 that year. I don't know how many times I had to reiterate that I did not "promise" we would not lose more than $50,000. He asked me what the actual loss was for that division and I told him I thought it was around $26,000.

He asked me to repeat that several times, as though he didn't believe that. I had heard him state during his opening argument that he had a expert who would show we had indeed lost more than $60,000. I told him I had no idea where that figure came from. I was reasonably sure my figures were correct.

During the next series of questions, we covered the areas of the company in which we were losing money. Again, I tried to offer a balanced view of what was going on with the company, which was not the purpose for which McDowell had me on the stand. Dang, I was bad at this—it was painful to sit up there and have to admit that we had lost more than $900,000 in the trucking division, and that we had lost a good bit of money in the Montgomery division. I didn't avoid answering that, I just wanted to balance it out with the positives. I knew I would get my chance when Brock questioned me later; I just had a tough time not being able to present a complete picture.

McDowell asked me about my refusal to get out of the trucking business because it was losing so much money. He also stated that Sonny suggested that we look at ways to divorce the trucking from the rest of the company, and that we had refused to look at that. We did vote against looking into that at the board meeting, but we were under contract with the tractor and trailer leasing companies and Sonny knew that we were in the process of trying to find ways to lessen the impact of those agreements. We told him to tell us how we were supposed to "divorce" the trucking division and he never came up with any suggestions, just that we should do it.

After the midafternoon recess, McDowell started another interesting technique. Instead of simply presenting the actual figures to the jury on prepared charts or graphs, he handed me a calculator and asked me to use it to give him some figures he wanted to present. Then he had me stand up and walk over to an unmarked chart in front of the jury and take various colored markers to begin drawing points and lines on the chart. I was standing within two feet of some of the jury members and even they seemed a little irked at this process. I even told Jerry that I would have been happy to prepare the charts for him, prior to trial, if he had just asked. Several of the jury members chuckled about that. McDowell asked me to put a legend on the graph to explain the different colors of the markers. I told him that I might have to charge him for these services…he told me to charge them to Brock.

The charts were designed to show the declining profits and increasing expenses for the company in a more dramatic way. I really don't believe that this was as effective as Jerry had hoped, even though the numbers were not good.

Then Jerry started asking about the "advance accounts" that the company had for various shareholders. He made the point that several shareholders had negative balances in their accounts, including me. As he had done in the interrogatories, he didn't want to acknowledge the disparity between the size of Sonny's account, more than $400,000, and the almost negligible amounts on all of the other accounts. Also, the company owed my mother more than $350,000 in her positive account. Their contention was that there was an agreement that those would only be paid back out of future earnings.

McDowell asked me whether I had ever written a check to pay back any of the $6,000 that I owed.

I answered, "No, I hadn't written a check, but that I had the company withhold some of my paycheck to pay back some of my debt." He didn't want to hear that, but it was true.

In what I thought was an interesting point, McDowell had me read a line from our audited statement in 1987 that said, "'The Company has advanced money to certain officers from time to time; there is no specified terms of repayment." I thought this was interesting because I had been told that in this sort of situation, the IRS would treat these advances as taxable income unless there were specific terms of repayment or signed notes of obligation. At least that is what our auditor, Gene Gibbons, had led us to believe. Gene had told us that each year he brought that note to Sonny—and Sonny never agreed to sign it.

The judge asked the jury to leave, then listened to arguments between the attorneys. He then called a recess until the next morning.

The next morning started out a lot like the day before. Jerry McDowell asked me about a business plan document which we prepared over the years using the SWOT method to evaluate the Strengths, Weaknesses, Opportunities, and Threats for each of the divisions. We had then attempted to plan ways to use the strengths and opportunities to attack the weaknesses and threats we'd exposed. Jerry asked me to give him the date of the report he had given me on the stand, and I spent the next ten minutes explaining what was in the plan.

I then began testifying about resolutions that we did have passed by our board which allowed me to borrow up to $100,000 without seeking board approval, and an unlimited amount with my mother's and my signatures. We did this because Sonny had done everything possible to thwart any effort we were making for refinancing, or even for capital improvements, specifically things like roof repairs. One of our buildings was leaking very badly, and even our banker agreed that it would be foolish not to fix that. We ended up fixing it out of operating funds, because Sonny blocked our efforts to get AmSouth to fund it.

During this testimony, I pointed out that Sonny had invited me to his house for discussions on helping us get financing for some things we wanted to do. This goes back to the meeting in which he said that, in return for 50 percent control on all of our decisions, a $7,000-per-month cash advance, and cash loans for his tax liabilities, he would use his influence with the banks to get us what we needed. This ended up being the headline in the Mobile Press Register the next morning.

Mobile Press Register	**October 17, 1991**
Fulton claims Callahan talked of 'influence'	

Then came one of the toughest "perception" problems of the whole trial. McDowell asked me to read one of the proposals Hudson sent to us during the negotiations. I'm sure this was hard for the jury to believe. This is the letter in which Sonny said he would accept $2,900,000 for his stock, or would agree to buy our stock for $3,800,000. How in the world could we say his stock was worth only $600,000, when he was supposedly willing to buy ours for $3,800,000?

I could just see the jury thinking, "Wow, that's a lot of money, I'd like to have that!" They seemed to believe that so much money was being offered to the Fultons, and we weren't even considering it. They must have assumed it to be worth a lot more, when actually the plain fact of the matter was that we neither wanted to sell out, nor did we believe Sonny could accomplish that payment. It was so hard to get across to the jury, and to the judge, for that matter, that just because someone wanted that amount of money, the majority is, by law, not at all required to purchase the minority.

We spent a good bit of time discussing the offers, back and forth, leading up to our largest offer, which was about $1,600,000. We withdrew that offer when we were told by the banks that we couldn't afford it and they would not support it. I testified that we even went further with a building swap and a combination note and cash deal on the table. I testified that after substantial consideration and number crunching, I realized we had gotten way over our heads in these negotiations. At that point, we just wanted to concentrate on getting the company back on its feet.

The latter part of the afternoon was spent grilling me about all of the problems we had with the banks concerning late payments and overdrafts. That was no fun either, but it wasn't something we had denied. As bad as the problems were, though, in later testimony from the bankers, every one of them expressed a desire to continue doing business with us and testified that they had never lost a penny to us.

Toward the end of my testimony, McDowell got into one of the quirks in tax law which caused both Sonny and my mother to pay taxes on revenue which was more than the audited profit of the company for the year 1990. Even though our audited statements showed a profit of only $5,101, the taxable amount was much more than that. Here's why: Sonny owed the company more than $30,000 in interest, which he did not pay. The IRS treats that as income to the company. The company owed somewhere around $30,000 in interest for the money my mother had loaned to the company. Since we did not have the cash to pay her interest, we were not allowed to write that off as an expense. Therefore, each shareholder had to pay more in taxes than expected. We declared no dividends for that year because we only showed the audited profit of $5,101.

McDowell blamed me for not paying my mother the interest due her, which caused an additional hardship on Sonny. We had also disallowed any further loans to pay these taxes. It would seem obvious, at least to me, that if Sonny had paid us his interest debt, we could have paid Mom's interest, thereby relieving him of that problem. Even more frustrating is that he was overpaid about $50,000 the previous year for taxes he didn't owe. It seems to me that he could have taken some of that cash and paid his "additional" obligation. This would be brought up again when we got to the last day of the trial.

There were a few more questions regarding investments I made in the Morgan Keegan account. The net effect of that was a loss of $70.

I was at the end of my testimony when McDowell brought up one of the strangest allegations of the whole trial. It accused us of using a letter from Steve Mixon of Ernst & Whinney, written in February 1989, to work a scheme in which we would declare only 50 percent of profits for dividends for five years, force Sonny out of the company, make five straight years of $400,000 profits, make Sonny pay the taxes on those record profits, then pocket $1 million in cash for which we would owe nothing in taxes. Danny and I were to be the beneficiaries of this while at the same time I was running the company into the ground and causing its insolvency...

That pretty much wrapped up McDowell's questioning of me. I really thought that I had done well under what I considered grueling attacks. I know very well that the process does not really allow the kind of fact-finding that I would have preferred, but I suppose most anyone who has been in that spot feels the same way. What was interesting, and what I hadn't anticipated, was the perspective I had from the stand.

I was trying to give the jurors the whole story all at once, which I suspect was a lot more challenging than it seemed. What I found most amazing was that I seemed to be connecting with them while I was talking. The eye contact was good and most of them seemed to be genuinely trying to listen. What was new to me was the small talk that went on in the hallway as we would take breaks. There was nothing of substance discussed, but I don't know how many times my brother and I were referred to familiarly as "you boys" by the jury members as we passed each other in the halls. They would say things like, "This must be hard for you boys," or "You boys must be looking forward to all of this ending." My parents felt the same camaraderie from the jury members.

At another time while I was testifying, I looked out into the audience and recognized a face that looked particularly out of place. It took me back a few years to my most active years in the Mobile Jaycees. When I was serving as a regional director, Mobile Chapter President Dennis McKenna and I had engaged in several battles featuring our differences on how the business of the chapter should be run. He was an attorney, and I just figured he had a few hours to spare and didn't want to miss his enemy being skewered. The first thought that ran through my mind was that he must really be enjoying this.

I really enjoyed Renee Busby and Garry Mitchell, the local news media who were there. We were very limited in what Brock would allow us to say to them, but I really did think they were trying to make sense out of a very complicated trial. I'm not sure they were as exact as I would have liked at the beginning, but I thought that their stories were fairly correct.

My mother took the stand late in the afternoon on Wednesday, after I had finished my testimony. Sonny had told anyone who would listen that he had initiated this lawsuit to "protect" Betty Jo from "the boys" who were destroying the company.

Maybe that line of thought worked with some people, but those who knew my mother knew it was ludicrous. Both of my parents cherished their family and would do whatever it took to fight anyone who would attack either of us. They were both furious, and Mom was determined to fight back. To some extent, that probably was not helpful as she testified on the stand.

Betty Jo Fulton was the quintessential Southern gentlelady, with an ability to communicate with people in a person-to-person situation better than anyone I've ever known. She would sit in her office and, one by one, employees, friends, and even perfect strangers would linger around in an informal waiting posture, looking for the momentary opening in her office. She was the "confidante" everyone wanted to have.

One thing that I found personally infuriating was that Mom had always been content to stay in the background when credit was to be given out for accomplishments. But that played right into the image that McDowell wanted to portray of someone who just went along for the ride. All of those years in which Sonny was getting credit, Mom was doing so many of the things in the background that are indispensible to one's success. She did that for all of us, and now she was having to defend whether she knew what was happening in our business.

When she was being questioned, she sometimes had trouble with dates and numbers she was asked to remember from the top of her head. But even Mom had to admit that the propensity to expound on our answers was a family trait she and I shared. The courtroom was amused quickly though, when Mom told Jerry McDowell to "hush, now" when she felt he was trying to bully her into some answer. It had already been a long trial, though, and even Kittrell said he was getting tired of hearing speeches from the Fultons. All in all, though, I was proud of the job she was doing. I do think she went a little overboard sometimes in trying to share the blame for some of my business mistakes, which were not any of her making. Sometimes that made her answers come off a little disjointed.

She was able to testify that there had been no "agreement" to pay 100 percent of the company's dividends "ad infinitum." She had also been the one over the years who was responsible for the tremendous success of our furniture leasing business, and she hadn't minded who got the credit, until now. She was famous for saying she'd watch the pennies, and you'd watch the dollars, and at the end of the day, she'd end up with the most success. The expansion I had so supported for the company was not especially her way of doing things, but she was supportive of our efforts to grow and willing to make the sacrifices to nurture that. She had certainly made sacrifices for Sonny to the tune of a difference of more than $700,000 in their personal "advance" accounts.

Jerry McDowell questioned Mom for the remainder of Wednesday and a good part of Thursday, trying to portray her as agreeing to "scheme" against Sonny in a conspiracy to force him out. Again she had to reiterate, time-after-time, that it was Sonny's desire to be bought out, and not ours to push him out. Nevertheless, after McDowell finished his questioning, Brock began his cross-examination. It was reasonably short, and allowed Mom to restate the fact that she would not have agreed to declare all of the company's profits out forever and ever.

The next witness on the stand was Joey Ginn, who we worked with at AmSouth Bank. His testimony was intended to reemphasize our strained relationships with the bank, and he certainly achieved that purpose. Sonny's attorneys brought several bank-related witnesses in to achieve the same purpose, but, with every one of them, Brock asked them if they had ever lost a penny from Finch or Tommy Fulton, to which every one of them admitted they had not.

Joey Ginn was the one witness with whom I did find myself surprised and exasperated. I had done my best to stay in touch on an ongoing basis with him, and to keep him well informed with the good and bad news from Finch. At one point, Joey testified that I had promised not to expand the trucking division any further than the twenty-six tractors we had under lease, until we could attain profitability. McDowell asked Joey if he would be surprised to find out that I had leased ten more tractors after I had made that promise. Joey sounded confused.

After Joey finished his testimony, I called him and asked him why he was so confused. I reminded him that I had informed him ahead of time that I was only refinancing an existing ten tractors under a new arrangement more beneficial to the company. He apologized and said he remembered clearly now, but that he had panicked on the stand and temporarily forgot. In my mind, though, this was just another strike against us, promoting the perception that we were secretive with the banks. We were not.

Sonny's lawyers proceeded to bring forth some expert witnesses over the next several hours, including one Lindsey Boney with Deloitte & Touche, one of the Big Six accounting firms. We had provided him with all the financial documents he needed to do his own analysis of the company. That is why I was so flabbergasted when he testified that we had lost $64,173 in the year 1988. This was more than the supposed $50,000 limit Sonny had imposed on the trucking division for that first year. You may remember how McDowell, in his opening statement, said that even though I had "promised" that we would not lose more than $50,000 in 1988 in the trucking division, his expert showed that we did indeed lose in excess of that. He further said that Sonny raised all kinds of objections to continuing the trucking division at the January 1989 board meeting because we had gone over my promised $50,000 limit. In fact, in my earlier testimony, I had stated that we had lost around $26,000 in 1988.

Brock turned to me during Lindsay Boney's testimony and asked me where his numbers had come from, and I could only answer that I didn't have any idea. They certainly didn't match mine. I looked closer at the numbers and realized what a colossal error Boney had made. He was reciting the cumulative numbers on a month-by-month basis to the judge and jury for the six-month period. He took the loss from July and added the August loss to that to come up with the cumulative loss for the first two months. This is where he started his mistake. He then took the cumulative losses, which were a running total at the bottom of the spreadsheet, and added those up, which meant he added the same numbers up multiple times. In other words, the Big Six accounting expert was off by about $40,000 in his analysis.

Now you might say, well, it was just a math error, and in the scheme of things did not amount to that much difference. I disagree. Sonny had maintained that he begged and pleaded with us to shut down the trucking division at the January 1989 board meeting, because we had lost more than the $50,000 "promise." How could Sonny have possibly known that Boney was going to make that error more than two years after that meeting? There were no such figures at the time of the board meeting, and the fact of the matter was that the trucking division was barely discussed at that meeting. In other words, Sonny just made it up.

I wanted Brock to really blast Boney for that, but, on balance, Brock was pleased with the testimony that Boney gave stating that he saw nothing wrong with the methodology used in the Ernst & Young report that the company had commissioned for the valuation of company stock. Further, he testified to the legitimacy of the "discounting" methods used to value minority shares and nonmarketability. On balance, he didn't want to discredit a witness he felt supported our side.

The next few witnesses were real estate appraisers whose testimony ended up having a dramatic effect on the ultimate outcome of the trial. Our argument, which I believe to this day was a legitimate one, was based on the fact that neither of these appraisals had anything to do with the value of Sonny's stock, either before or after the supposed devaluation charges levied at us. Furthermore, the comparables being used were not really comparable. Nevertheless, these guys were considered experts and their testimony would be damaging.

One of their theories relied on the "highest and best use" argument. Since they really couldn't find any warehousing companies in our area which had recently sold, they found a building in the size range, which was being used for manufacturing, and went with the theory that, if we sold the building to a manufacturer, it would be worth much more than as a warehousing facility. Using that logic, if we sold it to NASA, it might be worth even more...so what? The law clearly stated that we were not required to buy or sell our business, regardless of the value to the outside world. Now they were saying that we were under-utilizing our assets by being in the warehousing business. This was crazy.

I could go on and on with the fallacies in the appraiser's reports, but suffice it to say that they really should never have been introduced in the first place. They were introduced only after vigorous objections from Brock Gordon, all of which were overruled by Kittrell.

It was now Friday morning, October 18, 1991, and Sonny was to take the stand. Sonny was a seasoned politician and I expected him to put on quite a performance. He did, but not in the manner I was expecting. He seemed almost timid. He was so quiet that he had to be asked to speak up so he could be heard. Most of McDowell's questions were geared to establishing Sonny as the man who single-handedly built the Finch Companies and all of its predecessor companies. We never questioned his accomplishments, we just know he didn't do it all by himself. One of the most irritating points they kept making was that Sonny was responsible for all of the debts of the company because he had given his "personal guaranty" on everything. The inference was that he owed all of the mortgages and loans himself.

The fact was that my parents were as liable as he was for every one of those debts. Furthermore, if the property was worth anywhere near as much as he claimed, there was an overabundance of collateral. Also, it was no secret that he was already very highly leveraged personally, so there was no asset base any further at risk there, either.

We again had to hear Sonny talk about the $5,000 capital expenditure limit, which he said stayed in place for the first two or three years. That wasn't the way it really played out. I had kept up with that requirement for several months. After a while, I asked him if it was still necessary for me to run everything by him beforehand. He said it wasn't. In fact, he complained about us spending money refurbishing the office. When he saw the results, he said, "Well, we ought to upgrade the office every thirty years or so, whether it needs it or not." It had been a long, long time since any improvements had been made.

Sonny testified that he recalled my reporting at the board meeting in January 1988 that we had lost more than $60,000 in the trucking division. I love the fact that the only reason he "recalled" that number was because Lindsey Boney can't add. Then he said he brought that loss to the attention of the other board members and insisted that we stop the growth of the trucking division until that level of operation was profitable. While that may have been very good advice at the time, in retrospect, it simply never happened. This is another point I wish we would have pushed to show the jury that he often made up his "facts" to fit his needs.

I won't try to go point by point through Sonny's testimony, but there was a thread that weaved its way through his arguments. To this day, I'm not sure if he understood what he was saying, or if he just thought it made compelling rhetoric. The most pervasive was the idea that he was responsible for the company debt. I sincerely believe this was blown way out of proportion. In reality, I don't believe he would have ever been in a position to pay anything out of his pocket for the reasons I've mentioned before. First, there was always at least enough equity in the buildings to cover that debt, although not nearly as much as he insisted. Second, I firmly believe that my parents were in a much better financial position than he was, and they were every bit as liable as Sonny. But, time and time again, Sonny and his attorneys made it sound like he personally lent the money for the debt.

The next thing that his lawyers worked so hard to ingrain in everyone's thought process was that Sonny was the "only" one required to pay taxes on the profits of the company. That was a completely false impression. We had paid out substantially more in cash to all of the shareholders, including Sonny, to more than take care of any tax liabilities incurred from the profits we had earned.

One of the last things McDowell questioned Sonny on was his suggestion that we use an outside board of directors to run the company. We've always felt that was a disingenuous suggestion, since he was entitled to three positions on the board, and never once appointed anyone except himself and his son, Scott. It would have been interesting to see how things might have differed if he had put three outsiders in his slots.

Then, it was time for Brock Gordon to begin his questioning of the congressman. I thought one of the most important admissions Brock got from Sonny was that there was no written agreement regarding the required declaration of 100 percent dividends every year, ad infinitum. There was no agreement, even though Sonny says he would have never agreed to the 51-49 ownership split without that agreement. Brock also made it clear during his questioning that Sonny was never in a position to demand any more than a minority share.

Later in the testimony, Brock questioned Sonny about the fact that he had received more compensation for the years I was president than in the years he himself was president. I thought it was an excellent point, considering we were accused of making him poorer. I thought one of the things that would play well for our side was proving that Sonny had indeed received every bit of the money from his advance account that we had recorded. But it was like pulling teeth to get him to admit to receiving anything. Brock had a huge stack of checks, all written to Sonny's personal account or to pay Sonny's personal bills. One by one,

Brock got admissions that those were for Sonny's benefit, and not just conjured up by the Fultons out of thin air. Along these same lines, whenever the banks would ask any of us to report our personal financial statements, Sonny never included any debt he owed to the company.

Brock's next line of questioning was extremely revealing when it came to the valuation of Sonny's interest in the Finch Companies. The main crux of their argument against us was that we were offering way less for his stock than it was worth. In that part of his testimony, Sonny admitted to valuing his interest surprisingly closer to our numbers than to his. We were really feeling like we were making some progress in our arguments through Brock's questioning now. There were several periods of testimony in which Sonny seemed to really be evasive—and, I thought, uncomfortable. Then, almost abruptly, Judge Kittrell called for a recess until Monday morning.

The jury had seemed to be very attentive and we had been successful in maintaining eye contact with several of them, if not all. That changed dramatically when we came back into court Monday. Every one of us noticed it. None of the jurors were looking us in the eyes. In addition, there was a period of meetings between the judge and the attorneys on Monday morning, in which several arguments were being made regarding documents we wanted in evidence. When Brock and Alan came out of this meeting, they were concerned; it seemed to them that Kittrell had already made up his mind as to our being guilty to some extent.

One of the things we were going to be found guilty of was causing Sonny to pay taxes on income that was there because we had not physically paid the interest on my Mom's loan account to the company. Never mind that if Sonny had paid his interest to the company, we would have had enough money to pay Mom. At this point, though, Brock and Alan still felt like we were going to be successful against the other, more major charges.

The final period of questioning for Sonny concerned his written valuations of his interest in the Finch Companies. His testimony showed that on his personal financial statements to the bank, he had valued his interest at $450,000 in December 1984. Then, he valued it at $750,000 in 1986, and again, that same amount in July 1987. In February 1989, he valued his interest at $850,000. I really think this was important...after all, how could we have "devalued" his stock from the $450,000 when I took over, to the $3,800,000 he maintained it was worth now? It was so ludicrous; I didn't believe anything could be more twisted.

Brock was about to get back into the advance account reckoning when McDowell conceded that point. That was probably very smart, because his client was not handling that part very well. Their point was not that they were challenging the amount, just that it did not have to be paid back except through future earnings of the company. That then, for the most part, wrapped up Sonny's time on the stand.

The next thing we were going to hear was testimony from one of Mobile's greatest products, in my opinion. Joe Langan was a part-owner of Great Southern Corporation and one of the finest gentlemen I've ever known. He had served the city of Mobile as a city-commissioner for years, which, in our system at that time, meant he spent one-third of his term as the acting mayor. To this day, he remains one of the most respected of Mobile's leaders.

The point of bringing him to the stand was to let him testify that, only three years prior to that point, he had purchased a one-fourth interest in the Great Southern building for $150,000. He testified that he was a willing buyer purchasing from a willing seller, one of the tenets used by appraisers. This meant that if that was extrapolated to the other buildings, the values of all of the other buildings would have to be appraised at millions of dollars less than the estimates from our two expert appraisers. But even though that would have been a perfect "comparable" sale, neither appraiser used that value. In all fairness, they probably never knew about that transaction.

Dan Miller then took the stand for a short period to verify some of the accounting procedures used by Finch. He was ill at the time, and we weren't even sure he would be able to take the stand. We were grateful that he did.

Now it was my turn to return to the stand. This time, Alan Christian would be questioning me. I was really looking forward to this, because I wanted to clear up as much confusion and misleading testimony that I had heard over the past few days as I could.

Alan opened his questioning by allowing me to expose the positive side of what we had accomplished over the past several years, and in many cases allowed me to show positive comparisons with the previous administration. For example, I had never allowed the company financials to reach a negative net worth. That was not true of the years immediately prior to mine. We also addressed, in a very limited fashion, the fact that nothing in our records added up to the numbers put forth by Lindsey Boney.

We also wanted to show the tremendous growth in total revenue which grew from $2.7 million dollars when we took over, to $7.8 million dollars for 1990. We didn't gloss over the fact that we were struggling with the challenges that come with that kind of fast growth. We also wanted to demonstrate that my pay was not outrageous, as charged by Sonny and his attorneys. My compensation was less than Sonny's, even though I was managing a company which was almost three times the size he had managed.

One of the more important exhibits we wanted to go over with the court was one that showed the dramatic drop-offs in our obligations to the truck leasing companies over the next couple of years. It was precisely because of this that we were not jumping out there to shut down the trucking division until then. Our point was two-fold. With the lower costs of owning paid-for equipment, we might have had a chance to turn around the performance, or, in the worst-case scenario, be able to decrease and then shut down the division at a much lower cost.

During the next set of questions, we tried to clear up the misunderstanding with regard to whether or not I had been truthful in my dealings with Joey Ginn. He had testified on the stand that I had promised not to add any more vehicles to the fleet until we became profitable. That was the truth, and again we showed that we renegotiated terms on existing equipment.

Alan finished his questioning of me, and then Jerry McDowell got another shot at me. One of the first things he did was launch into that argument about my supposed purchase of ten new trucks after the agreement with Joey Ginn. He apparently believed his information on that transaction came from documents I had given to Lindsey Boney. Apparently, Mr. Boney didn't read those all the way through, either. After several accusatory questions, I think McDowell finally figured out that he was mistaken.

McDowell spent the next several moments trying to challenge my figures and argue that my charts comparing various financial statements and compensation results were not giving a real picture. But the more he argued, the more I felt he was losing those arguments. I really felt much stronger on the stand at this time than I had the last week. I knew my points were winning, but I just could not get a good feeling that the jury was even listening.

Alan had some great follow-up questions which allowed me to again point out that I had indeed been associated and working with Finch for most of my life, and also that we would again take a look at what to do with the trucking operations at the beginning of 1992. This is when the cost of operating and/or the cost of pulling out would begin to decline rapidly. This was a point we really wanted to get across to the jury. There was a plan. Then, except for a few questions from McDowell, my testimony was finished.

My mother went back on the stand for a few questions from Brock and McDowell, and that pretty much ended the testimony. Now the attorneys would begin launching into their closing arguments. This part of the process was really strange for us. It seemed that we were back in the ambiance of the opening arguments, in which the truth just went by the wayside. There was so much stuff thrown out there in such an out-of-context way that it seemed as if we had wasted an entire week.

McDowell went to a chart during his final argument and began to write down some figures, which, in essence, was a compilation of what Sonny and the appraisers claimed to be the value of the properties of the company. He went through several other tales about the "web" we had weaved, and how we conspired to force Congressman Callahan out of the company. It appeared to us that the jury was paying special attention to the numbers McDowell was pointing to on the easel, but it was hard to read the jury now. Ever since Friday it had become very difficult to get any eye contact with any of the jurors.

I knew that most of what was being said was untrue, and especially out of context, but I didn't know if the jury felt the same. We were hoping to get a good verdict from them because it had become obvious to us that Kittrell was very firmly in Sonny's corner.

Alan and Brock shared the closing argument duties, and I thought they both did a great job summing up the "real" facts. Brock spent a substantial amount of time arguing that there were many good years under my administration and, unfortunately, some tough times, especially with the trucking losses. He also made the point that just because a company loses money, it doesn't necessarily follow that the president did anything illegal, immoral, or unethical. I was so very proud of the summations, because I knew them to be true.

Brock was doing a great job pulling our arguments together when, right in the middle of his closing argument, Judge Kittrell decided it was time to take a break. We thought it was crazy to have to stop then, but it seemed typical of the way things had been going. Brock was able to continue his closing immediately after the break, but it did seem to interrupt the flow of his presentation.

McDowell finished up after the break with all kinds of demands, one of which declared that we should have to pay back all of the money that was lost in the trucking division. Can you imagine what would happen if officers of companies were required to do that when their good-faith efforts didn't perform? It would be total chaos.

The judge then gave some directives to the jury, or "charged" the jury regarding how they should make their decisions. He refused to give them some of our directives, which we felt undermined our ability to get a fair evaluation, but we still felt that we would come out fine. It was all very confusing though, so we had some real concern that the jury would not fully understand it all. We had the perplexing impression that the judge either could not communicate effectively, or was trying to communicate ineffectively to the jurors. But nevertheless they were then sent back to the jury room to begin their deliberations. Kittrell dismissed the jury and told them to be back at nine a.m. on Tuesday, September 22, 1991.

After the attorneys spent a substantial amount of time in the judge's quarters, they came out and told us that the judge wanted us to make one last effort at negotiations for buying out Sonny's stock. He had already made it clear to our attorneys that we weren't even in the ball park in what he felt Sonny should receive for his shares.

Later that Monday night, Brock, Watson, my mother, and I met with Sonny and one of his attorneys to discuss a buyout. We didn't go in there holding out any real hope, except that we believed that the jury was going to find in our favor, and that would tremendously weaken Sonny's hand. What we were not prepared for was the most obnoxious, obstinate attitude we had ever seen from Sonny. His price was not moderating at all, in fact, he seemed to be moving back up. We stayed at it for a while and then resigned ourselves to the fact that we weren't going to get anywhere that night.

Chapter Eleven
The Verdict

We showed up Tuesday morning to wait out the final deliberations and the jury's verdict. After that, we would find out where the judge stood on his decision. The morning started badly for us because, again, for some strange reason, we couldn't get the jury to look us in the eye. It was a drastic difference from their behavior prior to the weekend. Then we started getting some bad feelings from the questions that were being asked by the jury foreperson. Our attorneys were privy to those, and they came out and told us, "It doesn't look good, there is a lot of confusion among the jurors."

The court clerk read the verdict as follows: "We, the Jury, find in favor of the Plaintiff. We, the Jury, assess damages as follows: H. L. Callahan, compensatory damages, $2,927,500.80; punitive damages, $1 million.

$3,344,440.00, 49 percent stock; amount of the draw account, $416,939.26, which would make an award of $2,927,580.00, plus $1 million, for a total of $3,927,500.80."

The Judge then asked of the jury foreperson, "Let me just ask you about that, Ms. Manning, and you all tell me. You took the form of verdict that said Defendant, and you lined it out and you put Plaintiff in there because you wanted a form of verdict that said for the Plaintiff; is that—,"

THE FOREPERSON: I think so. Yes.

THE COURT: I mean, you did not intend to find for the Defendant,—

THE FOREPERSON: No.

THE COURT: —obviously, from the damages. That's so say you all? Unanimous verdict?
All right. Now, the other—I assume the figures on the left which say—is how you arrived at it?

[These were the figures taken from the chart McDowell used during closing arguments to try and establish value of the properties from appraisals, etc.]

THE FOREPERSON: Yes.

THE COURT: The 49 percent stock, was that the amount of the devaluation of the stock?

THE FOREPERSON: Right. That was the—the appraisal figures from the two, and

THE COURT: Okay. That's what those figures represent; is that right?

THE FOREPERSON: The jurors wanted it done that way.

THE COURT: Okay. I understand. All right. Read the other verdicts.

THE CLERK: Do you find from the evidence that there was an agreement to repay the Callahan account only out of future earnings of the corporation? Yes, Marianne K. Manning, Foreperson.

THE COURT: Now, it's got the figure twelve. I assume that means twelve jurors.

THE FOREPERSON: That's right.

THE CLERK: Do you want me to read that each time, Judge?

THE COURT: Yeah. Read that.

THE CLERK: All right. Are you reasonably satisfied from the evidence that the acts of the directors or those in control of the corporation are oppressive? Yes.

THE COURT: All right. You lined out illegal and fraudulent and put oppressive, and that's what you found—that they were oppressive?

THE FOREPERSON: Yes.

THE COURT: And the twelve represents the twelve jurors?

THE FOREPERSON: Yes, sir.

THE CLERK: Marianne K. Manning, Foreperson. Are you reasonably satisfied from the evidence that the corporation assets of Finch Company, Inc. are being misapplied or wasted? Yes, twelve. Marianne K. Manning, Foreperson.

THE COURT: Same there, twelve jurors?

THE FOREPERSON: (Nods)

THE CLERK: We, the Jury, find from the evidence that the following causes of action have been established: Waste and management [sic], corporate claim, twelve.

THE COURT: Twelve under the yes column?

THE CLERK: Yes, sir.

THE COURT: That's twelve jurors?

THE FOREPERSON: Yes.

THE CLERK: What's that word, reckless? Reckless? This word, is it reckless?

THE COURT: I don't know.

THE FOREPERSON: The word was—

THE CLERK: Wanton.

THE FOREPERSON: —wanton, wantonness. And some of the jurors had objection to that word and the definition, so they put recklessness.

THE COURT: Okay. Well,—

THE FOREPERSON: We didn't know what to do, and we've had to make so many—

THE COURT: I understand. And it's an involved case, and you've been attentive and I appreciate that. The problem is is [sic] that either there is wantonness or there's not under the definition of the law. And I can't accept a verdict that says reckless, because reckless is not the standard. Now—

THE FOREPERSON: We didn't know what to do. We just questioned what to do, and came out and asked questions and still didn't know.

THE COURT: Okay. Well, let's go on and come back to that. I'll let the Clerk read the next one.

THE CLERK: Intentional depreciation of value of all the corporate stock, twelve yes. In parentheses that says Callahan claim.

THE COURT: All right. I assume—let's see. Depreciation of all the stock. Did you find from the evidence that all the stock was devalued as a result of that?

THE FOREPERSON: Yes.

THE COURT: All right.

The jury went back into the deliberation room while we sat in absolute shock. It was as though we were living in some parallel universe. There was so much confusion, it was amazing. A few minutes later, the jury returned.

THE COURT: All right. Ms. Manning, I think I'll let you just read this time.

THE FOREPERSON: Oh, come on now. I don't have my glasses. Which part do you want me to read?

THE COURT: Well, read the whole thing, what you have.

THE FOREPERSON: All right. One of these papers you wanted me to correct the corporation part of it. It says: 'Of the total punitive damages assessed, we, the Jury, appropriation—I'm sorry, apportion the punitive damages as follows. And that's the one you wanted to mark the corporation off of?

THE COURT: Well, the corporation is not a Defendant. I assume that the damages—

THE FOREPERSON: Is against all of them. All Defendants, and I wrote that in, per se.

THE COURT: Okay. And the other one?

THE FOREPERSON: The other one: 'We, the Jury, find from the evidence that the following cause or causes of action has or have been established: Waste and management, twelve jurors, yes; wanton, twelve jurors, no; intentional depreciation of value of all the corporate stock—

THE COURT: Okay. You haven't changed any of the rest of it? Just the wantonness.

THE FOREPERSON: Twelve. No.

THE COURT: Okay. That's fine. Okay. That's the verdict of every juror? Unanimous verdict? Each and every verdict? Please indicate if it is your verdict.

Your verdict?

Your verdict?

Everybody's verdict?

All right. Ladies and gentlemen, we thank you. This has been a long and a tedious case and a complicated case, and we appreciate the attention that you've shown and your services to your State and County. And on behalf of your State and County, I thank you for your services. You will be discharged. If you will see Ms. Dawson, she has your checks.

We ask—well, we don't ask anything. I'll tell you this: Some people may want to talk to you about your verdict. You can talk to them, if you want to, or you don't have to talk to them; however you want to handle that.

Thank you very much.*

---

* I wanted the reader to see the jury verdicts and the judge's conversation directly from the trial transcripts, because it's almost impossible to explain the mass of confusion that had culminated from a week in trial. Also, I've included the jury form. It clearly shows confusion among the jurors as to what they were supposed to do.

Jury Forms

We, the jury, find in favor of the ~~defendants~~ *Plaintiff* :

Marianna K. Manning
Foreperson

We, the jury, *award* ~~assess~~ damages as follows:

H.L. Callahan

Compensatory Damages $2,927,500.80

Punitive Damages   1,000,000.00

~~Pinch Companies, Inc.~~

~~Compensatory Damages~~ _____

3,344,440.00   49% stock
− 416,939.26   Draw Acct.
2,927,500.80   Award
1,000,000.00
3,927,500.80   Total

Marianna K. Manning
Foreperson

Are you reasonably satisfied from the evidence that the acts
of the directors or those in control of the corporation are
~~illegal~~, oppressive ~~or fraudulent~~? (

Yes *12*

No ___

Marianna K. Manning
Foreperson

Are you reasonably satisfied from the evidence that the
corporate assets of Finch Companies, Inc. are being m applied
or wasted?

Yes *12*

No ___

Marianna K. Manning
Foreperson

We, the jury, find from the evidence that the following
cause(s) of action has (have) been established:

	YES	NO
Waste and Mismanagement (corporate claim)	_12_	_____
~~Wantonness~~ *Wanton* (both)	~~12~~	_12_
Intentional *↑ All the Corp. stock* depreciation of value of ~~Callahan's~~ stock (Callahan claim)	_12_	_____
Conspiracy (Callahan claim)	_____	_12_

d find against the following defendants:

		YES	NO
Thomas W. Fulton		_____	_____
Elizabeth J. Fulton	*12*	_____	_____
Daniel R. Fulton		_____	_____
Samuel C. Fulton		_____	_____

Marianna K. Manning
Foreperson

(TO BE FILLED IN ONLY IF PUNITIVE DAMAGES ARE ASSESSED)

Of the total Punitive Damages assessed, we, the jury, apportion the Punitive Damages as follows:

DEFENDANT   AMOUNT

Thomas W. Fulton   _____

Elizabeth J. Fulton   *all of the defendants*

Daniel R. Fulton   _____

Samuel C. Fulton   _____

Total $1,000,000.00

Marianna K. Manning
Foreperson

Do you find from the evidence that there was an agreement to repay the Callahan account only out of future earnings of the corporation?

Yes   *12*

No   _____

Marianna K. Manning
Foreperson

And that was that!

We stood up and everyone started leaving. Someone had mentioned that we had a judgment of almost $4,000,000 against us, and my dad said, "Thank God it wasn't $50,000...We could find $50,000." It was such a strange and out-of-character comment for my Dad to make. The numbers absolutely shocked us and simply made no sense.

When we were leaving the courtroom, Renee Busby, from the Mobile Press Register, approached me and asked for a statement. I told her, "We'll go back and look at all our options." I told her that an appeal was a real possibility. I also said, "I'm not sure the jury understood it all. I want our customers and employees to know we're still in business."

We hurried back to the company because we knew there would be a lot of concern from our employees about the future of the company. This was one of the toughest meetings I've ever led. I had a tough time staying composed while I tried to explain what had happened, when I didn't even understand it myself. Those who had fought so hard to make the company survive and at most times, prosper, were fighting mad. When you work that closely with people, they know your character. I really needed that from them, because our family had taken a huge blow. The vast majority of them would prove themselves as real friends over the years to come. A few wouldn't.

Renee would write in her article,

Mobile Press Register   **October 23, 1991**

[Fulton] said his family received tremendous support from their employees during the trial. "When you talk about the Fulton family, you're talking about the entire 130 employees at Finch, we all stick together."

...Callahan also asked Judge Braxton Kittrell to dissolve the company, which Thomas Finch, Mrs. Fulton's father, started in 1933. Kittrell took that issue under submission and said he will rule later.

The morning after the trial brought another strange occurrence. As though the trial wasn't screwed up enough, two jurors showed up at Judge Kittrell's office that morning and told the judge that what they read in the paper was not what they were told they were doing while they were in jury negotiations. Apparently Kittrell just told them that was too bad, they had voted unanimously for the verdicts, and it was too late to do anything about it now.

Somehow, our attorneys were made aware of the jurors' feelings about the results of their deliberations and how they believed they were misconstrued. The feedback we received from them told us a great deal about how they came up with some of the results. We were still amazed at some of their conclusions, but in regard to the "award" to the Callahan side, the following affidavits shed light on the confusion:

Affidavit of Valerie H. Wainwright

IN THE CIRCUIT COURT OF MOBILE COUNTY, ALABAMA

H. L. CALLAHAN,   )
)
 Plaintiff,   )
)
=vs=   ) CIVIL ACTION NO.
)
THOMAS W. FULTON, ELIZABETH) 91-001226-BLK
J. FULTON, DANIEL R. FULTON,)
SAMUEL C. FULTON, THE FINCH)
COMPANIES, INC., an Alabama)
corporation,   )
)
 Defendants.   )

AFFIDAVIT OF VALERIE H. WAINWRIGHT

STATE OF ALABAMA

COUNTY OF MOBILE

Before me, a Notary Public in and for said State and County, personally appeared Valerie H. Wainwright, who is known to me, and who, under oath does depose and say as follows:

   1. "My name is Valarie Wainwright, and I served on the jury in the above-styled litigation which rendered the verdict attached hereto as Exhibit A. I make this affidavit upon my own personal knowledge.

   2. In reaching the jury verdict presented to the court, it was my intention, and I believe the intention of a number of the other jurors, to establish a fair share value of the 49% of stock owned by the plaintiff in the event the Judge should decide on a dissolution of the Company. The $2,927,500.80 figure entered as

compensatory damages on the verdict form was the jury's valuation of the 49% of plaintiff's stock, less the $416,939.26 owed by plaintiff on the advance draw account. It was not my belief, understanding, intention or vote that this dollar valuation entered on the verdict form represented damages to be paid to the plaintiff. I did not intend or understand that plaintiff was to be allowed to keep his 49% of the stock in the company and to be paid the $2,927,500.80 amount as well. In point of fact, the foreperson of the jury declared during jury discussion that the value the jury placed on the stock was not a money judgment to be awarded to the plaintiff, but simply a valuation placed on the 49% of the stock by the jury. It was not my intention to vote for a money verdict against the defendants.

3.   The jury believed and voted unanimously that the actions of the Defendants were not wanton. In voting for the $1,000,000.00 punitive damages award, my belief was that this amount was awarded to cover court costs and attorney's fees incurred by the plaintiff. The jury arrived at the dollar amount of punitive damages by assessing a percentage of our estimate of the

fair share value of plaintiff's 49% of the company.
This approach was suggested by the foreperson of the
jury as a fair method of assessing attorneys fees and
costs.

4. In addition to our handwritten notes from the
Judge's oral jury charges, the jury forewoman, Marianne
K. Manning, brought in a small pocket dictionary which
was used to help us understand the meaning of some of
the terms used in the judge's oral jury charge and on
the jury verdict form. During the course of the jury
deliberations, different jurors asked Ms. Manning for
several word definitions including, to the best of my
recollection, the definitions of the words 'oppressive',
'conspiracy', 'waste' and 'wantoness'. Ms. Manning
looked up the requested words and read out the
definitions to the members of the jury. These
definitions were taken into consideration by me and the
other jurors prior to voting and filling out the verdict
form."

Further, affiant saith not. Dated this _12th_ day
of _November_ , 1991.

Valerie H. Wainwright
Valerie H. Wainwright

Affidavit of Kearney Windham

IN THE CIRCUIT COURT OF MOBILE COUNTY, ALABAMA

H. L. CALLAHAN,   )
)
   Plaintiff,   )
)
=vs=   )   CIVIL ACTION NO.
)
THOMAS W. FULTON, ELIZABETH)   91-001226-BLK
J. FULTON, DANIEL R. FULTON,)
SAMUEL C. FULTON, THE FINCH   )
COMPANIES, INC., an Alabama   )
corporation,   )
)
   Defendants.   )

AFFIDAVIT OF KEARNEY WINDHAM

STATE OF ALABAMA

COUNTY OF MOBILE

Before me, a Notary Public in and for said State and County, personally appeared Kearney Windham, who is known to me, and who, under oath does depose and say as follows:

1. "My name is Kearney Windham, and I served on the jury in the above-styled litigation which rendered the verdict attached hereto as Exhibit A. I make this affidavit upon my own personal knowledge.

2. As reflected on the verdict form, it was my belief, and that of one or more, if not all, of the remaining jurors, that the award of $3,344,440.00 for 49% of the stock was only the jury's opinion as to the value of the stock to be awarded Plaintiff if the Court or Judge later ordered a sale of said stock through those proceedings to be handled by the Judge or Court

alone. I absolutely did not understand or intend that the valuation of 49% of the stock was to be damages to Plaintiff to be paid by Defendants while Plaintiff kept his 49% of the stock. Nor did I understand that Defendants would be required to purchase the 49% of the stock for the amount found by the jury, unless the judge later ordered a sale of stock or sale of the company in that part of the case he was to decide. In fact, the foreman of the jury announced during deliberations that the value of the 49% of the stock was not a money value to be given to Plaintiff, and, therefore, I understood the amount of $3,344,440.00 was merely a valuation placed on the 49% of the stock by the jury. I did not intend to, nor did I vote for, a money verdict against Defendants other than as set forth as punitive damages.

3. The valuation of the 49% of the stock at $3,344,440.00 was intended by me and, I believe, by the other members of the jury to be merely the present valuation of 49% of the stock and not a money verdict against Defendants.

4. With respect to the $1,000,000.00 punitive damages award, I specifically and most emphatically state that I did not feel that the actions of Defendants were wanton, and the jury so voted unanimously. In assessing the punitive damages award, the jury

considered that Plaintiff was prejudiced by having to
bring this lawsuit, by incurring attorney's fees and by
the loss of revenues by the corporation."

Further, affiant saith not. Dated this _7th_ day
of _November_, 1991.

Kearney Windham
Kearney Windham

Sworn to and subscribed
before me this _1st_ day of
November, 1991.

Notary Public,
State of Alabama at Large

Supplemental Affidavit of Kearney Windham

IN THE CIRCUIT COURT OF MOBILE COUNTY, ALABAMA

H. L. CALLAHAN,   )
)
   Plaintiff,   )
)
=vs=   )   CIVIL ACTION NO.
)
THOMAS W. FULTON, ELIZABETH)   91-001226-BLK
J. FULTON, DANIEL R. FULTON,)
SAMUEL C. FULTON, THE FINCH)
COMPANIES, INC., an Alabama)
corporation,   )
)
   Defendants.   )

SUPPLEMENTAL AFFIDAVIT OF
KEARNEY WINDHAM

STATE OF ALABAMA

COUNTY OF MOBILE

Before me, a Notary Public in and for said State and County, personally appeared Kearney Windham, who is known to me, and who, under oath does depose and say as follows:

1.   "My name is Kearney Windham, and I make this affidavit to supplement the statements contained in my affidavit of November 7, 1991, in connection with the above matter.

2.   During the jury deliberations on the morning of October 29, 1991, Marianne K. Manning, the forewoman, read to the jury the definitions of at least two words from a small dictionary which she had with her. Two of the definitions I recall that she read were for the words 'oppressive' and 'wantonness'. After Judge Kittrell had given us his charge on the afternoon of

October 28, 1991, I was particularly concerned with the definition of the word 'oppressive', and I looked up the definition of that word in a dictionary I had at the office, Webster's New World Dictionary, 3rd Collegiate Edition. On the morning of October 29, 1991, during the jury's deliberations, I read to the jury the definition of 'oppressive' which I had obtained from the Webster's Dictionary. I believe that those dictionary definitions read to the jury by Mrs. Manning and me during the jury deliberations were taken into consideration by me and the other jurors and influenced us in our voting on the verdict in the above case."

Further, Affiant sayeth not. Dated this 12th day of November, 1991.

Kearney Windham
Kearney Windham

Sworn to and subscribed before me this 12th day of November, 1991.

John S. Bartley
Notary Public,
State of Alabama at Large

2436F(5-6)

You would have thought the whole trial would have been cast in tremendous doubt immediately, but we would have to wait to see how this would affect Kittrell's decision.

For the next several days and weeks, we spent a lot of time reassuring our customers and vendors. I remember so vividly the support from our customer base, especially the larger ones. Scott Paper was fantastic...we had developed a great relationship with them. Bill Wente, Bill Dollison, Keith Battle, and so many others were very kind to us and were a real pleasure to do business with. Bill Wente had a big concern about the product stored in our buildings, though, because of past experience with another of their warehousing vendors. Apparently, they were unable to access their product at that facility because the courts had chained all of the doors and would not allow access. I tried to assure him that this was not the same type of case; but, then again, I never would have believed that the lawsuit could happen to us in the first place.

Our staff at Finch continued to work diligently trying to turn around the unsuccessful portions of our business. The constant challenge to all of our people was to keep customer service a top priority. It was always our feeling that they would support us in the tough times, but only if we continued to provide the service they needed. I can't begin to express my sincere gratitude for the response from everyone at our "family" business.

I love being involved in my local community; but during these times, I sometimes wondered whether it would have been easier to be a homebody and avoid being out in the public eye. No such luck for me. In fact, on the Saturday during the trial, I spoke to the sales staff of McRae's, a clothing chain, on staying motivated despite setbacks. I had been asked to "motivate" them prior to their big fall sales campaign. Never mind that I had been in the paper every day that week with the trial. Actually, the speech went very well, maybe because, at that point, I really felt like we had the jury on our side.

The day after the trial I attended my Kiwanis Club meeting and got a lot of support from a good number of the members there. I know some of those people were friends of Sonny, but even some of them seemed genuinely sad about what had happened. We had untold numbers of phone calls and letters from people who were aware of how close our families had been. They were incredulous that this could have happened.

My Kiwanis club met every Wednesday for lunch. This was one of the oldest and largest Kiwanis clubs in Alabama, and usually had more than a hundred in attendance at their meetings. Its membership included some of the city's biggest movers and shakers, including Sonny Callahan. He rarely attended any meetings anymore. I'm not sure he was still a member. As luck would have it, I was the program chairman for the month of November. The first meeting as program chairman was fairly awkward. Everyone knew my family had just been saddled with a $3.9 million judgment. During my introduction of the speaker, I asked that we "pass the hat" to see if we could raise that in the meeting. It got a lot of laughs, but alas, no cash.

I was very active with the Mobile Chamber of Commerce and, as a member of their speaker's bureau, had been assigned a presentation to a local junior college. I didn't know anyone in the audience prior to speaking, but I was amazed at how mad they were at what they perceived from reports on the trial. Even though I presented the "Mobile, On the Grow!" chamber program, the question and answer period included several questions about the verdict. No one seemed to understand exactly what had happened. I couldn't really get into detail, but I asked them to stay tuned because I believed somehow it would all work out.

Another of my civic interests was my position as treasurer on the board of the Home of Grace for Women. On Monday, November 11, Doris Wood Littleton, who was the founder of the Home, and I had to appear before the United Way allocations committee. This committee was responsible for determining the amount of money to be distributed among the various agencies seeking United Way monetary support. Again, several of the people to whom we had to appeal were familiar to some extent with our case. I just tried to keep the focus on why we were there, not on our family's challenges. Everything went well and we received the allocation we had hoped for.

Tuesday would bring a great opportunity for the company to sell off the Montgomery moving branch. We had been negotiating with some folks there who expressed a willingness to take the building off our hands in return for taking over the division. They were already in the moving business and this would give them a coveted position as an Allied Van Lines agency. We weren't asking for any cash, just that they take over all of the obligations of the operation up there. The accountant for the prospective purchaser was a good friend of mine who had served as state president for the Alabama Jaycees two years prior to my term. Al Kelley fully understood that a moving company tends to lose money in the "off-season," and generally makes that back in late spring through early fall. This deal, while not bringing in cash, would immediately stanch the losses.

My father, brother, and I drove up that morning for a lunch meeting with Al Kelley and his client. She seemed very open to the idea as we went through early discussions, so we felt like the meeting would just be a formality.

Then, life went crazy!

At approximately 11:45 a.m., as we were about to leave the Montgomery office for lunch, I got a call from Watson Smith. What he said next was a bigger shock than the jury's verdict. In essence, Judge Kittrell had removed my father, my brother, and me from the company. As of that second, we didn't work at Finch anymore. Kittrell replaced me with Walt Hayes, who had retired from Scott Paper Company. Hayes was also one of Sonny's key fundraisers and a member of his congressional campaign finance committee.

We then had to go to lunch with Al and his client and explain somehow that we didn't work at Finch anymore, and therefore, we were not in a position to discuss what might happen in the future. Montgomery is about a three-hour drive from Mobile and you can believe that Dad, Danny, and I were in shock as to what was happening. Dad had already retired from Finch but had simply been working with us in his capacity as a consultant.

When we drove into the parking lot at Finch, Marcia Washam was right there. She was in tears. Marcia had been with Finch from the time she was in high school. We had seen her grow from someone who was painfully shy into a strong, dedicated, and outgoing sales leader. My first thought was that I had let down a lot of really great people. When I walked inside, I mentioned that I really didn't think I'd go out of town again if they couldn't even manage to keep our jobs safe!

We walked into my office where we found Walt Hayes sitting at my desk. There were two sheriff's deputies there waiting to serve us with papers. I moved past them and right up to Hayes and asked him to explain what was going on. He seemed very nervous, but made it clear that Danny and I were no longer employed by Finch. We were to turn in our keys and credit cards and would be allowed to remove our personal effects under supervision. We were told to return the next morning to accomplish that. It was one of the worst days of my life.

I tried to make it clear to Walt that we were juggling several balls in the air, and I would like to help him make sure that none of them fell. We had agreements with many of our vendors on when payments would be made. I had put together schedules for them and they had graciously agreed to work cooperatively with us. My concern was that Walt would just throw those out. I offered to help him access all of that on my computer (now his computer). He said that would be fine, but made no effort to allow me to show him how.

My father also tried to encourage Walt to use me to keep things going. Our impressions were that he was just letting us say anything we wanted, without acknowledging anything. We turned in our credit cards and keys and told him we would be back first thing in the morning.

The ordeal we were going through was tough for my parents. Not only were their sons thrown out, but my brother's wife, Angela, had to sit through the entire trial eight-and-one-half months pregnant. Now my brother would be without a job when Samuel Joseph Fulton was born on November 22nd, 1991. We did try to do everything we could to cherish and celebrate his birth, but Danny and Angela had to deal with a lot of extra stress. Nevertheless, I thought both of them handled it with class and courage.

After talking to our attorneys, we decided that all of us would meet at my parents' house that night. We all knew we were going to appeal all of this, the trial verdicts, as well as the receivership. However, Brock made no bones about it—it would be a long, expensive battle. One of the results of the court order was that all of the board members were removed and replaced by five members appointed by either the court or Walt Hayes. All of those were Sonny Callahan supporters. We were not even allowed one representative on the board of a company in which we owned fifty-one percent.

There was no doubt in anyone's mind that this was being done by Kittrell to force us into more favorable negotiations for Sonny's buyout. However, it wasn't couched in that type of language. In essence, the order turned over the control of the company from the majority to the minority. The court found that the Fultons had destroyed the "entente cordiale," when, in truth, that achievement was accomplished very successfully by Callahan.

The next day, Danny and I showed up to remove our personal belongings. The day before, Walt had said he would be there the whole time to observe us; however, he left us alone. Everyone in the company dropped by to tell us how much they hated the unfairness of the situation. I'd have to say their most-asked questions were, "How can this happen?" and "How can someone just take a business away from the majority and give it to the minority?" We assured them that we would fight as hard as possible to get it back. We just didn't have any idea how long that would take.

This thing had been so public that we just couldn't quietly hope it would get better. In fact, I was to introduce our Kiwanis speaker at the luncheon the day after I had been removed from Finch. I guess I could have easily missed the meeting, but I didn't feel like hiding. Our speaker was Doris Wood Littleton, the founder and leader of the Home of Grace for Women. I was very gratified with the moral support I received from my fellow board members and from Doris.

Everyone at the meeting was aware of the trial and that we had been removed from the company. I stood up to introduce Doris and laughingly made a joke about the previous remarks about "passing the hat" that I had made at the last meeting. I heard the same questions we had heard at Finch, "How can this happen?"

Even though we had been kicked out, I still made it a point to go to Finch most days to stay in touch with all of our staff, including the forklift drivers and truck drivers. I wanted them to know how much they meant to the Fulton family, and how hard we would work to get back with them. The support seemed unanimous, especially over the first few days. Bruce Byrd was especially helpful and would put himself on the line for us many times. I can't tell you how important his loyalty was to us.

Another key "insider," Mary Frances Hamilton, kept me informed constantly, sometimes several times a day. For the first few weeks, I visited several of our buildings and assumed Hayes knew I was there. I was a little surprised that I was being allowed to go there, but I'm not sure that he really did know what I was doing. I even made a point to stay in touch with all of our customers. Many of them were very concerned about whether they should stay with Finch or begin looking elsewhere. As I said, we had done everything possible to maintain excellent service to them, despite the cash crunch we had been fighting. I was also able to keep up with what was being said about us by Walt Hayes.

Before the trial, we had made a choice to put a woman by the name of Liz Forbis in charge of our accounting procedures. She seemed very organized and attentive to detail. She was visibly upset when we had returned from Montgomery as "former" employees. She said she would do everything possible to keep us informed of any and all changes to the accounting procedures. It took all of two days for her "loyalty" to switch. We were told by several allies that she immediately began telling the new regime of anything we were saying or doing. We immediately became very guarded about anything we did in front of her. Our receptionist, Cherie Still, did a lot to help keep us informed about who was coming or going, but after a couple of weeks, she also dried up as a source of information. I'm sure it was very uncomfortable for her. Out of a key staff of about two dozen, these were the only two who couldn't stand up to the pressure. The rest were amazing and throughout the entire ordeal, they put themselves at risk for us. My family will never forget their loyalty.

Brock Gordon, Alan Christian, and Watson Smith wasted no time in using the affidavits from jurors Kearney Windham and Valerie Wainwright to appeal to Judge Kittrell. On November 18, 1991, we filed a motion to stay Kittrell's order. They didn't feel like we had a chance, but we had to try this before we could move on to the next step. Nevertheless, our argument seemed solid and I really believed even Kittrell would have to pay attention to it.

Our plea consisted of asking for a new trial based on serious jury misconduct, confusion of the jury, inconsistent verdicts, failure to give requested jury charges, failure of the jury to follow the court's charge to the jury, and lack of substantial proof of plaintiff's case. Brock also made the case that removing us from the company would work a substantial, highly prejudicial injustice upon the defendants. We even agreed to allow a "special master" to oversee the affairs of the company to assure that there would be no damage to the plaintiff.

The attorneys for both sides met with Judge Kittrell on December 5, 1991 to discuss our motion. Reading the documentation of that meeting again illustrated the mass confusion, even from the judge, on what was actually decided. One of the most telling sequences was discussion about whether the remedy of receivership was proper or, in fact, extremely unfair and unnecessary. At one point in that conversation, Brock made his argument against Kittrell's order.

MR. GORDON: Your Honor, we are deeply troubled by the Court's order of November 12, 1991. We believe it runs counter to the business judgment rule and to all Supreme Court precedents. With respect to that order, I believe the Court has been deeply troubled by the fact the trucking business lost about three hundred thousand annually, and that Tom Fulton did not adequately explain to the satisfaction of the Court why Finch would stay in that apparently losing situation.

This and the other operating decisions which were complained about raised the question of waste and mismanagement and I know that's of concern to the Court. However, Your Honor, we believe that the Court should judge that in the context of the business judgment rule. And I would like to review that briefly with you.

It is well established without qualification that the majority has the right to manage the affairs of the company and that by operation of law the minority agrees to be bound by their decision.

In exercising the right to manage the affairs of the company, the business judgment rule operates to establish a presumption that the majority have acted in good faith. In the absence of substantial evidence that the majority acted out of fraud, bad faith, gross negligence, or ultra vires, the business judgement rule absolutely protects them...

THE COURT: But the jury so found.

MR. GORDON: ...from liability for their actions.

THE COURT: So the question is whether or not...

MR. GORDON: No, Your Honor. That's the problem. The jury was never instructed on the presumption to which the Fultons were entitled. The jury was never instructed that in order to overcome that presumption the [Plaintiffs] had to prove by substantial evidence that the Fultons had acted out of fraud, out of bad faith, out of gross negligence, or ultra vires.

And there is no evidence in the record, Your Honor, that would support any of those findings, even if the jury had been instructed as to those. There was no evidence...in fact, the evidence shows, Your Honor, and we talk primarily about the trucking business. The evidence is that Mr. Callahan voted in favor of getting into the trucking business. So, going into that trucking business could not—could not—be a basis to find that anything anybody did was in violation of the business judgment rule.

And the same thing is true about staying in the business. There was no evidence that anybody acted in an illegal manner in connection with the business decision that the majority has made to continue in that operation while they have been trying to find profitability.

THE COURT: When you are talking about in terms of ultra vires, I don't know that it is an ultra vires act. Perhaps not. But the account with Morgan Keegan was not within the ambit of the business that had been carried on. What about that?

MR. GORDON: Judge, on the Morgan Keegan, I really contend that that was just a deminimous thing.

THE COURT: I mean, there was no damage, or minimal, I agree with that.

MR. GORDON: Right.

THE COURT: But still it was done.

MR. GORDON: Judge, the testimony is it was permitted by the bylaws and the articles of incorporation. And there is no evidence to the contrary.

THE COURT: It's a complicated and interesting case. I have read the brief, and I've read what you're talking about about [sic] the business judgment rule. And I want to hear from you, but you don't have to repeat all the matters, you know, in the brief. I want to consider it.

MR. GORDON: Your Honor, we believe that there is no evidence that justifies or supports the extreme remedy that the Court has granted in this case. There is no precedent for the Court to take the majority stockholders of the corporation that's been in the family for...since the 1930s, and the grandfather started this business during the biggest depression this country has ever had, and now the Court is saying to the daughter and the grandchildren of that founder, look, you can't be an officer, you can't be a director...

THE COURT: Well, now, let's...

MR. GORDON: ...you can't be...

THE COURT: ...assume, though, that the findings of waste and mismanagement, and the statutory finding which permit this, the only option is to do that. Isn't it?

MR. GORDON: I'm sorry, Your Honor?

THE COURT: That's the only option—to remove them. You can't permit them to run the company when they're—if they're guilty of waste and mismanagement. The option under the statute is to dissolve the corporation.

MR. GORDON: Well, Your Honor, I think there are two responses to that. Number one, if you truly believe that these Defendants have done something that they shouldn't have been doing, that's not sanctioned by the business judgment rule, if you think—really believe that they've operated outside the business judgment rule, I think the Court's option is, one, to issue an order enjoining them from doing that act. That's an adequate remedy and the Supreme Court has said, if there is an adequate remedy, you should not dissolve a corporation.

So, one of the remedies this Court would have would be to issue an injunction against the Defendants, tell them, don't do it. And I can assure Your Honor that they won't do it.

THE COURT: What about that, David?

MR. QUITTMEYER: Judge, I think Your Honor would be issuing injunctions every day. It's just an impractical way of doing anything. The day Your Honor entered the order the Fultons were up in Montgomery trying to sell off a piece of the business. It would happen daily. The secret meetings would continue, decisions would be made and we would be before the Court every day.

The directors appointed by the Court are objective, they are charged with protecting the interest of all shareholders—Callahan and the Fultons. There is no favoritism in that. The Fultons still have fifty-one percent of the corporation. If the corporation makes money, they will benefit from that at the direction of the Board.

MR. GORDON: Your Honor asked what other remedy there is, I would like to address some other remedies that are available to the Court. The remedy that I think Your Honor has executed is probably the most drastic and the strongest remedy it could possibly do, contrary to the precedent of the Court and to the needs of this situation.

Something else Your Honor could do, I think, is appoint a special master. I think you could tell these folks to stop doing whatever it is you think they shouldn't be doing. I think you could appoint a special master and report to you on any aspect of the operation which is truly troublesome to the Court. That's certainly an available remedy.

The third thing that I think the Court can do—well, before I address the third thing, let me suggest to Mr. Quittmeyer that to suggest that what's going on now is equally beneficial to the Fultons and Callahans is, I think, ridiculous, Your Honor, when the Fultons have absolutely no say in what's going on, and Mr. Callahan has at least two directors, and I've forgotten how many he has the right to appoint under the...

And as a practical matter, in the real world we don't live in a fish bowl, the way it is now set up, as we have argued in our brief is, the Court, in effect has effected a majority squeeze-out. The company has been turned over to Callahan. And the Fultons have been placed on the sidelines. And that's not appropriate; there is no real basis for it.

Your Honor, I think there is something else that the Court can do. The Court can return this company to these stockholders. The Fultons would be willing to resign as directors, let Mr. Callahan resign as director, and let each of them appoint outside directors and run the corporation in that way.

If things require the attention of the Court, let a new suit be filed. But that would provide a mechanism for avoiding the very situation with the law which now exists that the law simply says is a greater evil than the one which was there before.

And I think this would provide a mechanism for the corporation to operate in a dispassionate method with outside directors making the important policy decisions of the corporation and proceeding hopefully in a manner back in profitability as this company has enjoyed lo these many years, and return to the stockholders the fruits of some sixty years of labor.

And we ask the Court to consider that.

THE COURT: Is that something the Plaintiff would agree to?

MR. MCDOWELL: You're asking us...

MR. QUITTMEYER: Judge, we can't respond to that right now. That's the first time we've heard anything about that.

THE COURT: I understand. I mean, your client is not here.

(PAUSE)

THE COURT: You know, I'll say it again, I've said it before: This case should have been settled. Have you all explored that anymore?

I mean, I'm not afraid to rule. I'm not afraid to go ahead and bring it to its final conclusion, but, I mean, there are a lot of complicated and serious issues in this case. Have you all talked anymore about settlement?

MR. GORDON: Judge, we made a proposal to the Plaintiff. We will continue to pursue it. We've told the court all the way through this thing that the Fultons want to settle this case. We have told Your Honor that they want to pay fair value for Mr. Callahan's shares. We have proposed to the Court...

THE COURT: Just for what interest you have, I never thought that the offer was a fair offer that they made based on my evaluation of the evidence. And, you know, I sit impartially. I don't care one way or the other.

MR. GORDON: Judge, I understand the Court has that feeling about it. And the Defendants don't believe that Mr. Callahan's offer is a fair offer.

THE COURT: He offered to pay them a million more than they agreed to take, that's pretty...

MR. GORDON: Judge, he could have offered to pay three million more and it wouldn't make any difference. That doesn't establish...

THE COURT: Well, they stand now in a position to lose everything they have. And I don't understand why they wouldn't be willing to talk settlement.

MR. GORDON: Well, Your Honor...

THE COURT: I don't know what the extent of it and I really don't want to get into it.

MR. GORDON: Yes, sir.

THE COURT: I just encourage both of your—not just your, I'm encouraging the Plaintiff as well...

MR. GORDON: Your Honor, let me respond to that, though. Because I think the Court has, perhaps, a mistaken impression that the Defendants have their heads in the sand. They don't.

THE COURT: I'm sorry. I didn't understand.

MR. GORDON: I said I think the Court may have the mistaken impression that the Defendants have their head in the sand about settlement. I can assure you they don't.

THE COURT: I don't know. I just said that based upon the offers that I heard, I did not think that it was a reasonable offer which they made to him for his stock.

MR. GORDON: Well, Your Honor, it was based on the Ernst & Young report, which was an outside...

THE COURT: Well, very candidly, I didn't think very much of that report and the jury obviously didn't either.

MR. GORDON: I agree with Your Honor, they didn't. I agree with that. And we have offered, as Your Honor knows, to have that whole process repeated.

THE COURT: Well, have you all talked settlement recently?

MR. GORDON: Yesterday.

MR. MCDOWELL: There was a proposal made to me yesterday afternoon that totally ignores the fact that there is a verdict in this case, in my judgment. And I have not had a chance to talk to Mr. Callahan about it, but I told Brock that I certainly would not recommend what he suggested to me yesterday because it ignores the fact...

At that point Kittrell called a private, "off-the-record" conference with the attorneys, and the session ended.

While I had already been offered employment opportunities, I remained adamant that we would settle all of this soon and I would be back in charge at Finch. But I was very grateful to those who offered their help. Judging from the transcripts above, our case seemed very strong to me. But what was painfully obvious was that Kittrell would have to admit to being wrong (or stupid) in order for us to get any relief. I guess that's the fallacy of asking a judge to reverse himself. Also obvious was the fact that he was doing everything possible to empower the Callahan negotiations. I don't believe for one moment that he was an impartial or uninterested party in that negotiation.

We weren't surprised that Kittrell ruled in favor of himself and Callahan. That doesn't mean we weren't very, very disappointed. It appeared that we were now in for a long, expensive appeal. Sonny's attorneys kept saying they wanted to find a way to settle, but the verdict and the "award" made settlement virtually impossible. They reminded us at every turn that they had a $3.9 million judgment, even though the value of Sonny's shares did not magically increase just because Kittrell and the confused jury said so. We were not going to put ourselves in a position of spending the rest of our lives in indentured servitude so that Sonny could get what he wanted. Even if we had wanted to, we would only have ended up driving ourselves back into court eventually; so really we would never have been able to settle on his terms.

Chapter Twelve
Outside Looking In—the Appeal Period

I continued to visit the Finch offices and warehouses, which really irritated Walt Hayes. I enjoyed making him uncomfortable, even though he was never as uncomfortable as we were. Thankfully we had so many allies still in key places at Finch, and they kept us well aware of all that was happening. In fact, it almost became a "Hogan's Heroes" type of operation in which I took on the role of Hogan while Hayes was like Colonel Klink—at times, it was absolutely hilarious, even if it was simultaneously tragic. For the time being though, I was entitled to view all of the financial documents of the company because I owned at least 5 percent of the Finch Companies' stock. I was able to pull various documents into an empty office and begin perusing through them. I was fully aware of everything going on thanks to our insider allies; but we didn't want Walt to know that was how we were being informed, so I would use these sessions to cover ourselves.

Our "spies" were getting us more information than you could imagine. Much of the information we received was gleaned from Walt Hayes himself. He had met with Judge Kittrell the day before we were thrown out. As he described it to others still at the company, he was to meet with Danny and me and advise us that he was appointed by the court to carry out its directions, to manage the company, and to generally be "in charge."

Walt's statements and attitude made it clear that this was not to be a temporary fix, even though that is what the public was supposed to believe. Hayes's actions clearly showed it was his intention to hand over the company to the Callahan side. Instead of some sort of temporary receivership, the intention and effect of Kittrell's order was to turn the company over to the Callahan side.

Hayes first called Carl Jones at First Alabama Bank and told him about the situation, and that Walt's signature would now be on our checking account. He explained that there was no intent to dissolve the company, but to make it a more profitable business. He did the same thing with AmSouth Bank.

The feedback we received from the key employees regarding Hayes's first meeting with them was interesting. He told them, "I've been appointed by the court as CEO of the Finch Companies and am completely in charge and responsible to the court. My intention is to make Finch stronger and more profitable, and more enduring than ever."

Hayes went even further, "I need your help and your absolute loyalty to me and the company, and no one else."

He then met with the rest of our employees and made it clear to them that he was "in charge" and that they were to recognize him as the only one "in authority." Again, he insisted on loyalty to him only.

His next quest was to meet with the union shop steward to explain that he was in charge and to assure them that he had no intention to "de-certify, bust up, condemn, or criticize the union and the employees." This was very noble of Hayes, except for the fact that the union had de-certified itself several months prior to this time. It's another indication of how out-of-touch Sonny had been. It was obvious that Sonny was advising Hayes on his every move.

Now Walt was prepared to meet with my mother. He explained to others that as long as she was cooperative and recognized him as the "boss," she would be allowed to stay. Otherwise, she would be thrown out. Mom, as feisty as ever, told Hayes, "Well, we'll just see about that."

When we showed up that afternoon, the meeting was very tense. He had instructed us to come the next morning and remove our personal effects. When we showed up the next morning, we had a short conversation with Walt, after which he left. We were alone for a couple of hours.

When Walt returned, he seemed annoyed that I took all day to accomplish the task of clearing out. I explained to him that I wanted to be consulted and to contribute. He was not receptive at all, choosing to just ignore me as I tried to explain the key parts of the operation.

After I left the office, Walt went to Liz Forbis and Louise Cotton and told them to tell me that "these records are no longer available."

He acknowledged that I was trying to be helpful, after all, this company and our people meant everything to me. While they (the court, Sonny, and Hayes) didn't agree with me running it, I was maintaining a delicate balance with vendors and customers and with the support of a great bunch of employees, and I didn't want anything detrimental to happen. Throughout his discussions with our employees, he referenced many conversations with Sonny Callahan. To add insult to injury, the new company lawyer for Finch was David Quittmeyer, Sonny's trial attorney.

Walt had let it be known that he would hire an "assistant" who was to be a "gopher-type." He appointed a gentleman who had also retired from Scott Paper. Howard Sumrall came aboard and, I'm sure, just wanted to do what he could to help the situation. My mother told us about her first meeting with Howard and that he didn't seem to be possessed with the level of arrogance we had seen from Walt. In fact, she told him in one of their early meetings that once he really saw what was going on, he would be ashamed of his part.

At some time, weeks after that meeting, Howard told my mother that he was indeed disgusted with what he saw. He offered to resign, but my mother urged him to stay on. We really wanted someone who could objectively see what was happening. From that time on, Howard was an ally of ours and, to the best of his ability, tried to protect my mother from some of the more harsh treatment and threats. All of the Fultons owe a huge debt of gratitude and admiration to Howard Sumrall.

On Friday, November 22, 1991, I confronted Hayes about his decision to violate a loan agreement we had with Presidential Finance. While I didn't particularly like the factoring arrangement, it was our only option at the time. My family had placed our personal guaranties on that agreement, and Hayes's actions had put us at extreme risk. I chewed him out pretty thoroughly, during which time he explained to me, with a deluge of profanity, that he disagreed with them and he felt no obligation for the company to honor our agreements. Even Bruce Byrd told him after I left that he had gone too far and that kind of language might get him in trouble. Nevertheless, I got a call from Brock Gordon shortly after I left regarding the confrontation. He suggested that I call Walt back and apologize. Brock didn't want the judge to ban me from showing up at the office.

One thing we had always prided ourselves on was the fact that we never missed a payroll. We were not even late. I started getting all kinds of calls from our employees on December 5. Apparently, our owner-operators were paid one day late, and the rest of our employees were paid six hours late. One of my competitors said that he saw a huge group of our truck drivers gathered on the street and the parking lot between two of our buildings. They were not in a good mood, according to him.

Walt noted to our "spies" that the personnel seemed unhappy with the late payroll and that some of the salaried personnel did not behave properly. It still amazes me that he didn't seem to understand that we had a very good relationship with these folks, and that he had earned absolutely no respect nor loyalty.

With the exception of Liz Forbis and Cherie Still, we felt that we had the absolute support of the rest of the staff, from top to bottom. Mary Frances Hamilton called me virtually every night at home and gave complete reports of all that she saw. Bruce kept me constantly informed also. Bart Ray and Ed Alexander kept me apprised of everything going on in the trucking division. Bart was supportive but would always get worried that Walt would find out that I was visiting with him, as the trucking division was located in separate buildings from the main office. Ed was much more combative.

I really felt bad for the rest of the staff, too. They worked so hard putting in extra hours and extra effort which was not compensated in pay. They are just good people. Some of them were treated like dirt, but never gave up. Marcia Washam, Louise Cotton, Ed Alexander, and Kim Welch were just some of those who were heroic in their ability to stay strong during this period. Marcia had grown so much in the years previous to the takeover—now she would benefit from her toughness. Louise and Kim were habitually harassed by Walt.

Ed Alexander had the distinction of being the only Finch employee to be fired twice in a week from the company. Walt apparently got fed up with Ed challenging him and fired him on December 19. Ed had been a hard worker and, in our opinion, a valuable employee. My mother hired him to work at Furniture Leasing Concepts the next day. That news got back to Walt quickly and he ordered my mother to fire him again. She refused, and apparently chewed out our CEO.

Eventually, we had to give in and let Ed go, on the advice of our attorneys. Before that, though, we had prepared a statement for a very public press conference in case Hayes fired my mother. We never delivered it but boy, would it have been powerful! That's probably why our attorneys vetoed it.

Here's that press release that would have been given by my mother:

Today's events, with regard to me and my family, have come about for one reason—those in Congress don't have to play by the same rules as average taxpayers. They make laws and regulations which control our lives and promptly exempt themselves from them. Our situation is a perfect example of this.

Four years ago, Sonny Callahan began an underhanded, sleazy campaign to terrorize those members of his family who dared to question his insatiable demands for cash from the operating capital of the Finch Companies, Inc. At the time he was asked to slow down his spending, he was receiving $10,000 per month and an additional $30,000 per quarter for taxes. These were loans which were supposed to help him adjust to life in Washington, DC. Congressmen have different living standards than you and me. In December 1987, without informing the Company, who was to pay for it, Callahan sought and received advice from the corporate attorney, Tom Hudson, on how minority shareholders could sue the majority, and how, in effect, to "...cause a variety of problems for management by protesting everything..."

While Mr. Callahan claims that the chief cause of the problem was the losses in the long-haul trucking division, there existed no long-haul trucking division at the time he had these clandestine meetings with corporate counsel. However, these meetings do coincide with the period of time when Callahan's demands for cash were highest. It was only after repeated requests for slowing his "borrow and spend" activities, and our concern that up to 50 percent of the corporate profits remain in the company, that he began to use his program of harassment. We first noticed the change at the January 1988 board meeting, following a record profit year for the Finch Companies, Inc. Sonny questioned everything possible at the board meeting, but refused to visit the company to learn more about what went into the financial statements and the changing operations. This board meeting lasted six and one-half hours that night, and did not conclude until May of that year, after a total of more than eleven hours. Again, Sonny refused to visit the company except for board meetings, which he began taping.

While we rarely saw or heard from Sonny in the last six
years, except as we worked in his campaigns, he built up a debt
in excess of $400,000 over the amount of substantial dividends
provided him by the company. He refused to sign notes acknowledging this debt, nor did he make any efforts to pay this debt,
except through the hard work of the employees of the Finch
Companies, Inc. During the trial, Sonny admitted that he had
not paid income taxes on this debt, which is clearly required by
the same tax code he expects you and me to follow. But, then
again, congressmen don't have to obey the same laws that they
set for the rest of us.

When the Company ran into hard times, instead of pitching
in to help, Sonny demanded that we buy him out at exorbitant
rates. While he listed the value of his stock in his personal financial statements as $850,000, he demanded $3,800,000 from
our family or else he would sue us in court. Oddly enough, those
same financial statements neglected to mention that he owed
any loans to the Finch Companies, Inc., even though you and I
would be charged with fraud and liable for up to $1 million in
fines and up to thirty years in jail. But, congressmen don't have
to live by the same rules as you and me. In addition, he would not
settle for any of our offers which would require him to pay taxes.
With today's economic times, and with some of the difficulties
our company was fighting, you would hope a congressman would
pitch in and help. But, that would be hoping for too much in
this case. Sonny's response was to refuse to visit the Company's
operations, except for formal board meetings. His only other response was to demand that we shut down the trucking division,
without ever offering to sit down and look at the ramifications.
Ultimately, his response was to sue his family—those of us who
had always supported him, in the worst of times.

My actions today may seem extreme, but maybe it's time for
extreme action. My family is being held hostage by a congressman, whose combination of greed and power has blinded him to
sense of fairness and compassion.

Furthermore, an unprecedented enforcement of receivership
has thrown my two sons out of work, leaving their wives and
eight children without income. The receiver and all of the directors on the board are allied with Callahan, leaving my family
with no representation, even though we own a majority of the
stock. We have asked for and are entitled to a rejection of these
decisions, or failing that, at least a new trial.

Again, my family has been terrorized almost beyond belief and the Company severely damaged. Why has this happened? Is it because my family hasn't earned enough in profits to add to the exorbitant pay and benefits provided by taxpayers to our congressman? Is it because only a congressman would tell you and me that they have had to lower their living standard by moving onto a yacht? Or is it because congressmen don't have to live by the same standards as you and me?

I would be happy to take your questions at this time...

My guess is that would have been a powerful press conference.

On December 20, 2001, Kittrell gave us the right to choose two board members. We had to do so no later than December 24. The Callahan side had substantially more time in which to choose their representatives. We asked Steve Mixon, who agreed to represent us immediately. I also asked Arthur Outlaw, who was a very respected former businessman and had served as mayor of Mobile and chairman of the Alabama Republican Executive Committee. He considered it, but turned us down because of poor health and at the insistence of his wife. I really don't blame them...it would be a very stressful position. I did get an appraiser friend and tennis partner of mine, Jim Cochran.

Steve had always been a fighter, and although constantly frustrated, fought hard to protect our interests. He had the advantage of being involved with Finch for a decade or more. Unfortunately, Jim did everything he could, but was badly outnumbered. Because he was not as intimately familiar with the history of the company, his position was made almost impossible. I will always be thankful that he agreed to take on this burden. Eventually, he would resign and we would ask Billy Kimbrough, a well-known attorney, active with the Democratic party, to represent us on the board. His reputation as a bulldog was especially helpful, and we were very grateful for his help.

Bruce and Mary Frances continued to provide us with Walt's musings and good information on everything behind the scenes. I particularly got a kick out of Walt's concerns about the Fulton family.

> Tommy Fulton was in demanding to look at books, financial statements, payroll, etc. and to use empty office. I advised him that he could see the financials and all other records "upon written demand, explaining the purpose to do so and requesting a reasonable date that this could be done." He wrote on paper that "Walt Hayes refused to allow him to see financial statements etc" Not true – above is what I told him...

Here's a great story from January 2, 1992:

> ...Confrontation with Tommy on financial records and use of office. He did not accept that he had to write a letter requesting records. My voice became strong and office heard conversation. I advised him to get a letter! He refused. I left for an appointment at Scott. He left a little while later taking 10 months cost reports.

Here's my take on that meeting. I was sitting in the office he mentions, already reviewing some of the documents. I already knew where everything was, so I didn't really want him to "get" them for me. In reality, I had several other ways to get the documents I wanted. Nevertheless, this was one of the most comical confrontations I've ever had. I was sitting at the desk, pushed up next to it so that I really couldn't move much. Walt started turning beet red (he did that a lot), and made a step toward me while standing almost directly over me. I thought he had lost it and was about to swing at me. In order that I would be able to move quickly, if necessary, I scooted my chair back a few inches. I've never seen anyone jump so high in such a confined space. That's when he started ranting and raving that I didn't have the rights to anything and that he was calling the judge. Then he stomped out of the office.

Later, Bruce told me that Walt asked him if I owned a gun, and if I was crazy enough to come back and do something drastic. He and I laughed. I really enjoyed those moments in the midst of all this injustice, but I really thought we would eventually win. I just liked making Walt's life a little uneasy.

Here's another confrontation from January 9, 1992:

Tommy in & raised hell—threatened people in all areas with dissolution of company and they out of jobs in 30 days—bad scene—took 2 hours of meetings with personnel to calm them down.

That's not really how it came down. One of the supposed purposes of the receivership was that the company be dissolved. It is not supposed to just take over and, in essence, give the company to the minority at the expense and detriment of the majority.

———————

In a Mobile Press Register article by Renee Busby, the head-line stated:

> **Mobile Press Register**   **January 10, 1992**
>
> New trial on Callahan suit refused

This was the ruling we knew Kittrell would make, and Renee wrote, "in his ruling, Kittrell states that the directors of the corporation are to present to the court within 30 days 'a plan with a view toward liquidating the corporation in a fashion most advantageous to all the stockholders.' "

It was, in fact, Sonny Callahan who had asked for the dissolution of the company in his lawsuit. It was also a threat from Sonny's attorneys, which was used time and again to try to force us into some kind of settlement. In fact, in a letter from Jerry McDowell to Brock Gordon dated December 11, 1991, McDowell stated that "we are convinced that on a dissolution of this company that Sonny would wind up with more money than what you are offering us in settlement."

The plain fact of the matter is that over the next few years it would become obvious that the values they had placed on the company were never close. They were grossly over-valued. If the board had been able to come up with a real value for the company which was anywhere near Sonny's valuation, they would have sold it or even dissolved it immediately.

Walt expressed his views often with others at the company. He let them know that he felt my mother was losing control of the situation out at Furniture Leasing Concepts. He said that he had a good meeting with her, but was skeptical of her abilities.

This was laughable. Mom had built that company from scratch and did such a great job that two national chains left Mobile rather than continuing to try to compete with her. One of them introduced my mother at a national convention as the lady who ran him out of his own hometown. Of course, the following discourse from Hayes after that meeting might give a hint of how she perceived him:

> BJ (Betty Jo) informed me that she "hated my guts and everything about me" but will try to focus on business—not personalities...

We were in negotiations in an effort to perform a split-off of some sort with the different parts of the company. The attorneys were handling all of those discussions, and we were kept abreast of the progress, or more truthfully, the lack thereof. Sonny's proposals weren't even close to what we could accept. In several instances, his deals would keep us intertwined, and after this experience, we weren't willing to get into a situation open to future litigation. It had to be a clean split. In addition, throughout the talks, we were reminded that they had a "judgement."

Even though we were continuing to negotiate, it was becoming obvious to us that we were in for a long, drawn-out battle. As long as Sonny and his attorneys harped on the "jury award" of almost $4 million, a reasonable settlement was out of the question. It seemed ironic that everyone involved felt that there had to be some kind of way to get the parties to settle, but the biggest obstacle came about because of the jury's misguided and confused verdict, and Kittrell's endorsement of that verdict.

Toward the end of March 1992, negotiations had basically reached an impasse. David Quittmeyer sent a letter to Brock telling him that the sheriff would be dispatched to take possession of my Finch stock certificates. This was supposed to start the process of satisfying what was now more than $4 million in judgments, including interest. Indeed, my six-year-old son, Finch, answered the door at our home and ran to Lane, telling her there was a man with a gun outside.

After they seized my stock, they proceeded to seize each of the Fultons' shares, excluding my mother's, Lane's, and Angela's, one at a time. I suspect they enjoyed the drama of it all. Brock had attempted to have Kittrell stay this order, but we were denied. However, Kittrell did seem to bar Callahan from selling or pledging our shares. What it did, in effect, was give Sonny any dividends declared on that stock, even though a victory on appeal, on our part, would have left us in a position of trying to get our rightful shares back.

In a meaningless but amusing gesture, Danny had taken Sonny's shares out of the vault and kept them in his "custody" during the whole period of the receivership. We didn't even have to get a sheriff's deputy to get it.

One of the things Sonny wanted to happen was the sale of the trucking division. The board and Walt Hayes did eventually find a buyer/investor for Finch Distribution Systems (FDS). That was really not surprising, but what was very strange was who the buyer was for FDS. In a Montgomery newspaper story, written by Bill Poovey and dated May 17, 1992, the headline read,

---

Mobile Press Register   **May 17, 1992**

Officials see no conflict with their link to firm

The first sentence said, "Alabama's revenue commissioner and an assistant, who takes over the top job Monday, said their links to a new trucking company do not conflict with their department's work enforcing some trucking laws." James Sizemore would be leaving as revenue commissioner to take a job with the Alabama Development Office, which would allow Whit Guerin to take over his job. They both said they didn't have anything to do with the new venture, called Partner's Freight Company. Instead, Sizemore's wife would be running that entity. At first, according to this article, Guerin denied having any stock in the company, but then admitted that he was an investor, but was in the process of divesting himself. It might just be my imagination, but this whole thing stunk, at least a little.

Our appeal to the Alabama Supreme Court was filed on June 12, 1992. It would be a long period of time, much longer than we thought possible, before we would hear our answer. If we had known exactly how long it was going to take ahead of time, I'm not sure we would have been able to stomach it.

What made this period of time additionally frustrating was that while we were completely out of power, Walt Hayes's actions caused my mother and me to be personally sued by at least one vendor, and threatened by others. Unlike the period before we were thrown out, no vendor or banker had been able to say they had ever lost a penny from the company or us individually. As tough as times got, we always paid our debts, albeit sometimes very late. Now Hayes had violated that promise and just told us that the judge would take care of it. Sonny constantly complained that he had personally guarantied the company's debt, but we had never put him in this situation.

It was equally frustrating that we were getting no credit for the negotiations we had begun with several of our trucking equipment vendors to improve our ability to turn the trucking division around, or to put it in a better position for disposing of the equipment in a systematic way. We had built excellent, profitable divisions in warehousing and furniture leasing, and we expected to benefit from the closing of our moving divisions in the 1992 fiscal year. The results for 1992 were very good, as we expected. I'm sure Sonny's board members and Walt Hayes believed that they were solely responsible for the dramatic turn-around. I credit the superb work of the staff who actually did all the work.

I can fully understand that the Callahan- and Kittrell-appointed board members felt that they were doing all of us a service. Furthermore, because I was never allowed to speak to them directly or explain the reasoning behind things that I did, I don't believe they ever really got a true picture of what positive things we had accomplished. That's not really their fault. But this is the reason it may come off as ungrateful, on my part, that I don't spend a lot of time crediting them with the turnaround.

However, when it comes to Walt Hayes, I can honestly say that the turnaround came about in spite of him. He treated many of our best people with contempt and disrespect that would not have been tolerated in most any other operation. More than once, some of the women in our company were verbally abused, including my mother. Thankfully, these were very strong women who learned how to stand up to him. These included but were not limited to Marcia Washam, Louise Cotton, Kim Welch, Betsy Swinson, and Lynn Miley. Our accounts payable clerk was our best "spy." She called me at least once a day to let me know what was going on at Finch, or just to shoot the breeze.

This is not to say that the guys working there weren't also fantastic. I can't mention Bruce Byrd's name too many times for what he did to keep things together. If there is a hero with regard to keeping the Finch Companies alive and thriving, Bruce would be that key person.

There would be some interesting items that we saw from the board minutes. At the December 1992 meeting, Walt estimated a profit of $450,000. He also asked that the board approve a dividend payment to the shareholders that would allow them to pay their tax liabilities from the profit. Later, at the February 1993 board meeting, Walt admitted that the profit was around

$297,000. He then said that the shareholders were overcompensated, but the board apparently just said that was fine. Hmm...I believe that the inability to accurately project estimated profits and losses was a major criticism of my administration...!

Another of the criticisms of me was that I wouldn't get out of some of the leasing contracts. For one thing, I had given my word, by signature, that I would honor those contracts until such time as they would agree to allow me to get out through mutual agreement. When the government took over our company, the judge just simply gave an order saying that Finch was out of the contract. We still had to weather several threats on our personal guaranties. In at least one of those cases, an appeal court overturned Kittrell's decision, and the vendor was allowed to recover on a letter of credit. I can just imagine how the courts would have treated us if we had attempted to do what Hayes and Kittrell did.

Chapter Thirteen
New Career in Real Estate

Since we knew our return was ultimately going to depend on our appeal to the Alabama Supreme Court, we knew that it was time to start looking for an alternate means of income. I had to get a job. I wanted to do something that would allow me the freedom to move back readily into the company and, at the same time, do something that could be integrated into the Finch Companies. Again, we believed that somewhere down the road, some level of competent jurisprudence would see the travesty that had taken place.

There were still major battles to fight, but it was time for me to "hunker down" and earn some money. I picked up the phone and called Marie McConnell, who was more than gracious and supportive. She had built a very successful real estate company and had been recognized as Top Realtor in the state of Alabama before starting her own firm. That's the reason I had suggested that Scott Callahan spend a year learning from her.

I told Marie up front that I wanted to learn the residential real estate business so that when we finally got the Finch Companies back, we could open our own brokerage. It's a sure sign of confidence and class that allows someone to train her future competitors, and I have always appreciated her willingness to do that, not only for me, but for several of her agents. I had dated Marie's oldest daughter, Angie, in high school, so I had known her for years. In fact, my parents lived next door to her and her husband, Jack.

I began my license classes at Marie McConnell Realty's school. It was an eight- to ten-week process taught by Elaine Sessions, one of Marie's agents, and it used videotapes to go over the fundamentals. There were about eight or ten others taking the class at the same time. One of these was a lady who had recently left work at the courthouse. She said that she worked in a position that gave her a bird's-eye view of our trial. She also said that everyone she knew down there believed our case was a travesty.

I received my license in April 1992, and began working as hard as I could to get started. I knew a lot of people, but on the other hand, a lot of people knew I had just started in the business. Getting your license and earning a living in real estate are not all that closely related. One of the best ways for new agents to get started is to do phone duty. As people drive by your company's listings, they call to get information, set up an appointment, and even see if you can help them sell their house. Most of the calls have to do with showing a specific listing. One of my first opportunities came from a young, newly married couple who wanted to see inexpensive homes. They asked me to make up a list of those and set up some times for me to show them. His dad had agreed to help them with a down payment and closing costs after they found the home of their choice.

I don't know if it was because I was new at the job or if they just weren't sure what they wanted, but we had soon looked at more than thirty or forty homes. They finally found one they loved and invited his dad to see it for himself. It was the longest day of my real estate career. We crawled up under the house, through the attic, viewed every square inch of the house and ended up sitting in the den while the son and dad argued about the wisdom of purchasing this home. After a few hours, I had to make the observation that if we were going to spend any more time in the house, we were going to have to pay rent. By the end of that afternoon, no one was speaking. The deal was dead, and they would postpone looking for a while.

At our sales meetings, Marie stressed the importance of acquiring our own listings. From a realtor's standpoint, it was more lucrative to list a home than to spend all of your time driving around showing others' listings. I definitely wanted that first listing.

One of the most hilarious listing opportunities I had came about as a result of phone duty. The son of the owner of a property had wondered what we could do about selling his father's vacant house. (You experienced realtors have already picked out the myriad problems I was about to encounter.) Eddie Craddock, an experienced realtor, offered to go along with me as an advisor. I was happy to take him up on his offer.

To say I was desperate for my first listing was a huge understatement. I thought this was going to be my day. As soon as we drove up to the property, Eddie said, "Forget it, you don't want this listing!" The son let us into the house, which was a picture of absolute disrepair. We walked into the bathroom and looked through an eight-inch gap next to the tub, all the way to the ground under the house. Still, I would not be deterred.

The son told us to go to his dad's house just around the corner and tell him what we thought we could do about selling that house. I should have paid more attention to the fact that the son would not be accompanying us. Again, Eddie said, "Leave it, you don't want this listing." And again, I told him I was getting this listing...I wanted my first listing, no matter how bad it looked.

As we walked up to the screen door, we heard barking. Big dogs...at least two of them. I knocked on the door and a guy yelled out, "What do you want?" He made no effort to calm the growling canines and barely let me get words out of my mouth before he started cussing. I could hear Eddie behind me...way behind me, saying again, "Let's go!" I conceded that discretion would definitely be the better part of valor. I think Eddie thoroughly enjoyed relaying this experience to our fellow agents at the next day's sales meeting.

I did finally start getting some listings, and some sales, which I hoped would be a relief to my parents. Their support in helping us keep our kids in their schools and making sure we were able to feed our families was invaluable. All of us were thankful that my parents were in a position, though very stressful, to allow us to fight for our return to the company. We were fully aware that most people would have had to throw up their hands. I'm sure that's what Sonny and Kittrell were hoping for us to do.

As I said, things started coming together a little bit for my new career and I was starting to see some progress, and some commission checks. I began to dearly love going to the closings at the title companies. However, I still needed to string together some successful deals. My goal was to make the million-dollar club in my first year. It's hard to measure that milestone against today's numbers. Nowadays, it's not unusual to see agents closing over two million in a single month. Nevertheless, I had put together what looked like a very successful eight- to ten-day succession of closings, one right after another.

I was very excited to go home and tell my family, especially my wife, that we were about to have the biggest success of my fledgling career—four closings in an eight-day period! Then it started happening. First, I got a call telling me that one of the closings jumped the track and the buyer could not meet the loan requirements. It turned out that he was still married, his wife was in France, and she would not give her permission. It was the smallest of the four, so while I was upset, I was still able to tell Lane that the three biggest were still in line.

That was until I received another call from a title company telling me that the next buyer had been unable to meet their requirements. This was a much bigger deal, but I still had two more closings lined up. I don't even remember the reason for the third failure, but it really, really hurt. I didn't even want to tell Lane about that one, but I assured her that even though that one fell through, the biggest one was still on schedule. That one deserves an explanation of its very own.

I had taken this particular call from a lady who was anxious to move out of a rental home she shared with her husband. She described the kind of home she wanted and I set up several appointments based on her wishes. She and her husband were both employed at a large, local manufacturing plant, like many folks in the area, and had more than enough income to qualify for the price range in which we were looking. When I picked her up to show her homes, her husband was not present. She told me that he had said to pick out whatever made her happy and he would go along with her wishes.

I had pulled up about eight listings, most of which were listed by other real estate brokers. But one of them sounded familiar. It was a Prudential listing priced at $119,900 located at 6666 Hounds Run Drive. I knew that Marie McConnell Realty had a listing on that street at one time, but the computer printout clearly showed that it was a Prudential listing. When I drove up in front of the house, to my surprise, it had a Marie McConnell sign in front of it. I figured there must have been a mistake on the computer, so we went on inside. She immediately fell in love with it.

There was another oddity on the listing printout. The printout said that it was a four-bedroom home, and this house clearly had only three bedrooms. We did notice, though, that the master bedroom seemed extra large. We felt along a ridge on the wall and realized that apparently, at one time, there was an extra door which had been covered over, and the room enlarged. It didn't matter, three bedrooms was just fine with her! This was her dream house, and she wanted it now.

We hopped into the car and began the drive to her house to write up the offer. As we rounded the corner, I noticed a house for sale on my left...with a Prudential Real Estate sign in the front yard. One quick look at the address and I almost choked—6666 Hounds Run Drive S. Whoops...I had shown her the listing at 6666 Hounds Run Drive N. To muddy the waters even more, the house she wanted was actually listed for $129,900, substantially more than the one I had the appointment to show.

It didn't matter, she still wanted to buy the other one and was willing to offer full price. That was fine with me, and after a quick tour of the "real" listing, we headed to her house to write up the offer. I met her husband and offered to take him to see the home they were about to purchase, but he declined. I should have noticed a few things during the offer, but I was so excited about the sale that I accepted her explanations. When it came time to put her name on the purchase agreement, she took a few minutes to decide what that name would be. She then explained that she and her "husband" were not technically married, but had been together for more than twenty years. They would both sign as responsible for the debt, so I didn't get too concerned.

I took her to a mortgage company she had requested from a list of several I had recommended. She asked me to sit in with her, which I did. After a preliminary discussion, the mortgage representative felt that there was more than enough income to qualify and, assuming everything came out as she portrayed, it would get quick approval.

Then I got the news. After three of my deals had fallen through, the final insult came. My customer had given bad checks for both the credit report and the earnest money, had four different social security numbers, and had bad credit under both names she was using!

Dang, this was a bad week. Dinner at home did not taste very good for a few days. Lane and my brother's wife, Angela, were working at Furniture Leasing with my mom, so at least we were getting her check every week. But this was a huge blow to my ego. I had really had enough blows by then.

I had to reassess my goals regarding the million-dollar club. My new goal was to achieve my million dollars in successful closed sales before I had a million in signed but unsuccessful closings. I made it in my first eight months with a $50,000 cushion. I didn't have the time to make my mistakes over an extended period of time, so I had to make them quickly.

I was honored to achieve the Top 100 Realtors status in my first full year as an agent. There were about one thousand realtors in our association, so I was in the top 10 percent. Over the next few years, I was asked to be part of an orientation panel for the Mobile Area Association of Realtors. I figured that was because I had made more mistakes faster than most realtors. Maybe the new folks could start on making a whole new group of mistakes, bypassing the ones I had already made for them...at least that was the theory.

I met some incredible people during those years with Marie McConnell, and I really appreciated the professionalism I witnessed among the vast majority of realtors in our area. While I didn't particularly care for the reason I got into the business, I still cherish the relationships I developed and always will appreciate the tremendous support I was afforded. There is always a positive aspect to every negative situation, even if you don't get there by choice.

Chapter Fourteen
Win of the Appeal...We're Back!!!

We had been waiting for what seemed like an eternity to hear something from the Alabama Supreme Court. It didn't seem like you could tell very far in advance when your case would be heard. Finally, we got some news. We were told that a decision had been made and we all gathered to await the results.

It was fairly confusing in that the Supreme Court, after forty-three pages, stated that their decision both affirmed in part and reversed in part the results of Kittrell's decision. The main decision meant that we would get a new trial. It did not get involved in any decision to remove the receivership, however, and that was terribly disappointing.

We had appealed the original case on several different points, but the Supreme Court apparently needed to look no further than the jurors' use of the dictionary. We were thrilled and anxious to get a new trial scheduled. But we had substantial concerns about going back into Kittrell's court since it was obvious to us that he was anything but impartial.

Nevertheless, it was gratifying to see the headlines in the April 17, 1993 edition of the Mobile Press Register:

Mobile Press Register   **April 17, 1993**

Callahan judgment reversed

Our attorneys had advised me to limit my discussions with the paper, but I was quoted as saying, "We're pleased with what we've seen so far. Obviously, we have to have time to digest this. It looks to me to be as much of a victory as we can hope for now..." Privately, we were jumping for joy.

We found out eventually that the new trial date was scheduled for September 27, 1993. There would be a lot of preparation needed to make sure that we presented our case in a clearer manner. The constraints of a courtroom make that very difficult; but at least now we could see that, among other things, Judge Kittrell's failure to allow our attorneys direction of some of the jury "charges" had led to the jurors' confusion.

I didn't know how we were going to get a judge to treat us fairly, but at least we had a chance. Also, without the "award," maybe Sonny and his attorneys would be more reasonable about negotiating.

We weren't going to let it stop at that, though. Brock helped us file a lawsuit against Sonny Callahan in which we alleged that he engineered a conspiracy to take over the company. To us, it was painfully obvious that Tom Hudson and Sonny sat down together and put together their plan to make life miserable for the majority, and by doing so, force us to buy Sonny out for substantially more than he was worth. When that didn't happen, the minority shareholder lawsuit, in effect, gave Sonny the company. We weren't going to just be on defense this time. That got in the Mobile Press Register on July 30, 1993, with the headline:

Mobile Press Register   July 30, 1993

Relatives hit back against Callahan

Negotiations on splitting up the Company began again in July. We now used the "you cut the pie, I'll pick the piece" method of negotiating. There was just one major stipulation that we had: Furniture Leasing Concepts (FLC) was to remain with the Fulton side of any deal. My mother had built that from scratch and we just felt letting it go would be a travesty. Unfortunately, that would prove to be unworkable.

Once they understood that we would not give up FLC, Sonny and McDowell basically cut the pie very closely around that piece. Eventually, Mom told us that she did not want to stand in the way of getting a deal done, and offered up FLC. It broke our hearts, but Mom was always one of the most personally unselfish people I've ever known.

One of the things that made negotiations so difficult was that Sonny still owed the company more than $300,000 and Finch owed my mother more than $300,000. Any attempt to cut the pie fairly got skewed because of these debts. Also, McDowell kept mouthing off that they had a $3.9 million dollar claim from the first trial and we were ignoring that fact.

The trial dates began to be more fluid with dates continuously delayed, since Kittrell seemed desirous of letting us try to work out a compromise and split up the company. Nobody really wanted to get back into the courtroom. Nonetheless, the attorneys on both sides were forced to continue preparing for a possible trial.

We eventually came to a preliminary agreement which would require me to get refinancing to remove Callahan's name from any remaining Finch Companies debt. In fact, under our agreement, he would have no debt. That meant that I would prepare a business plan and go back to AmSouth Bank asking them to underwrite this agreement. They very patiently listened to my proposal, then unceremoniously turned us down. I had to weather a few insults along the way. I tried a few other local banks, but got nowhere with them. I started to sense a real problem. If we couldn't get financing, the deal falls through and our concern was that Sonny would end up with the whole company anyway. It was September 1993, and we couldn't get financing.

Bruce Byrd was still keeping me well informed on the atmosphere at Finch and Walt Hayes's take on all of this. Walt told Bruce that there was no way the Fultons were going to get the warehousing company back, because there was no way we would get financing. Walt knew that I still talked with several people out there, but he believed that Bruce was on his side. This led to some funny antics along the way. We did get Bruce to tell Walt that we were negotiating with banks all over the South. We knew this was driving Walt and probably Sonny crazy.

We were still having some meetings with the attorneys from both sides, and the questions we were being asked affirmed that our planted stories were being heard. Jerry McDowell even asked me if I had told people that I was going to run against Sonny for Congress. I had jokingly told that to someone, knowing they would pass it along.

On November 4, Judge Kittrell appointed a mediator to help with the Fulton and Callahan negotiations. Frankly, I'm not sure this guy helped, but then, maybe I just didn't see what he contributed. Kittrell just seemed to want this tar baby off his hands. I don't blame him.

Finally, we got a break. Steve Mixon suggested some insurance-related lenders who specialized in commercial real estate. The first one we met with seemed very interested, but we couldn't quite get them aboard. The second one was a thrill. Their office was located in the same building, right next door in fact, to Sonny's congressional office in Mobile; their entrance doors shared the same internal hallway. So when I went in to meet with Richard Brinson of Camp & Company, who was affiliated with Businessman's Assurance Company, I had to sneak in without being seen. It was hilarious. I would turn the corner, look down the hall and dash into Richard's office. We were virtually sure that if Sonny knew where we were looking, he would do or say something to mess it up.

At the same time we were trying to get this done, the Finch Companies was still trying to resolve a lawsuit in which they had become involved earlier. When Hayes sold the trucking operation to the Partner's Freight group, he had apparently not been forthcoming to them. Well, as hard as it is to believe, they sued the Finch Companies, which was represented by Walt Hayes, the receiver, for misrepresenting several assertions promised during the sale.

On November 10, 1993, we received great news from Richard Brinson. Businessman's Assurance (BMA) gave us a loan commitment for the refinancing. We just had to come up with $33,000 for loan application and origination fees to make it happen. We also had to come up with a stand-by fee of $54,000. These had been fairly lean years for the Fulton family, but the company still owed my mother a substantial amount of money. Sonny opposed the company fronting that money, even though it was fully refundable upon the closing of the loan. In order to get the money refunded, closing on the loan had to take place no later than January 19, 1994.

We had been operating all this time under the assertion that we had a bona fide agreement with Sonny on the split-off. He was fully aware that we had put more than $30,000 of my parents' money at risk, as required by BMA, and did not object at all. However, in early December, McDowell was stating that there was no agreement, and they began to make demands for additional cash. This was so frustrating. This madness was the reason we could never come to agreement years ago—every time we thought we had an agreement, Sonny would continue to add to his side.

This was taking much longer than I had imagined. Richard Brinson was doing his part to get extensions on the loan closings, but I had to believe that BMA was getting a little tired of this being dragged on and on. However, the final closing date was set for February 28, 1994. There was a lot of last-second maneuvering, but we finally closed on the loan on February 28 and would regain our positions at the Finch Companies on March 1, 1994!

We were getting strong indications that Walt Hayes was doing some things that were not exactly proper. Our "spies" were telling us that he was prepaying some of the expenses of the Callahan side of the deal with Finch Companies money. There would be expenses that were the responsibility of Furniture Leasing Concepts that Hayes was paying ahead of time from the Finch Companies checking account. Also, I had been made aware that Walt was planning to take some furniture out of our Montgomery branch and maybe elsewhere. In fact, he did take the furniture from Montgomery for his own use. Unfortunately, we weren't really able to do anything about these injustices, since Kittrell wanted to avoid involvement in those aspects.

We had been staying in close touch with the folks at Finch during all of this time. They had been so wonderful and supportive and we would have gone crazy without their support. I know they were under a lot of pressure, and they weren't required to do the things they did for us; my family will never forget how much their support meant to us.

One of the most gratifying phone calls I ever made in my life was when I called Bruce Byrd and told him that the deal was going through and we would be back out at Finch. He was thrilled and wanted me to tell him the exact moment I would be coming out to tell Walt. He wanted to be in Walt's office when I showed up. I called him when the deal was done and told him we would be taking over in March. I would be coming out there to begin setting up the transition.

Bruce was in Walt's office when I arrived. I went directly to Walt and told him that I was there to begin the transition and he should waste no time getting out to FLC, where I assumed he would be taking over. Then I sat down in my brother's office, which was next door and unoccupied, and did everything possible to keep from laughing out loud.

Bruce told me that Walt had no idea that we would have been able to get the financing and asked Bruce if he thought I had been successful. Then he called Quittmeyer and asked him what he knew. These were some of the truly sweetest moments of my life. I went around to the others and shared the excitement with them. They were thrilled.

Liz Forbis was not particularly happy, but everyone assumed she wouldn't be staying on at Finch. We knew she would be leaving with Walt and Sonny. Our receptionist was the other one who had turned on us, but I think she assumed we didn't really know that. She was always pleasant, but we knew where she placed her loyalties. On the first day that we were back, I went up front and told her that she would probably want to head on out to FLC. She said she wanted to stay, but I told her I thought she would be more comfortable with the Callahan side. She left immediately.

On the other hand, Walt never really got around to pinning down who was going to stay on at FLC. It was unanimous... everyone got up and left to go to my parents' house. We were not allowed to encourage them to go with us, but there was never any doubt that they would go with my mother. The next day, they all came out to Finch and applied for a job—and all were hired.

The loss of FLC was not just a huge sacrifice by my mother; it was a sacrifice for the staff who had built it. Most of them knew nothing about the warehousing/trucking industry, but they remained loyal to our family. Lynn Miley began working in the sales area. Betsy Swinson became our controller, and Debbie Henderson worked in the clerical area. Everyone was aware that there was a three-year non-compete in place and that, the second that time was up, we would re-open a furniture leasing business. I'm sure Sonny believed the same thing.

As luck would have it, our challenges weren't quite over yet. Betsy was a very meticulous controller. Her attention to detail was legendary. Betsy was famous for having what we called the "willie" factor. If someone gave her the willies, we knew there was something wrong with them. I know it's not scientific, but it seemed to work.

As we settled in and began to move into a more normal mode of operation, Betsy began to say that there was something about our accounts payable clerk that gave her the willies. We assured her that she had been our best spy, and was infinitely loyal to us. She had called my house almost every night in the first year that we were gone, and frequently even while we were waiting out the appeal. No way could she be a problem. But Betsy kept insisting.

We should have noticed the signs quicker, but it wasn't a sure thing until one Saturday, when my mother and Betsy were trying to figure out some discrepancies in some of the bank statements. Mom would oversee the books and her experience in watching the pennies was invaluable. The two of them confronted the clerk about some questionable checks, and while faced with the clear evidence, she admitted that she had been writing some checks to herself. She admitted to doing it for only a short period of time. As we later discovered, she had actually embezzled more than $160,000 over almost four years, at the rate of $2,000 to $4,000 a month! In fact, it started just before we were kicked out of the company, and continued, unabated, all the way through the receivership.

When she was tried, the judge (not Kittrell) was so ticked off that he sentenced her to two years in jail. Her attorney tried to offer restitution in place of incarceration, but the judge was incredulous that somehow she would be in position to pay it back within her lifetime. I think the judge realized how hard we had struggled financially, and was as disturbed as we were that she would steal this money at the same time she was supposed to be paying our bills. It was just a little while later that we found out another judge, without our knowledge, gave her probation and required restitution. To this day, we receive around $200 per month from the courts. I'm not even sure that pays for the interest, but I guess that's just the way things work.

Over the next several years, the Finch Companies enjoyed tremendous positive times and very challenging negative times. That's the nature of business. I still had more lessons to learn, but that's the nature of life. The good news is that on March 1, 1997, we built a 32,000-square-foot shopping/office complex which included a location for my mother to get back into the furniture leasing business. It is a source of great satisfaction that it became very successful and that she managed it daily until her final illness.

Chapter Fifteen
Lessons Learned

There are so many stories out there about family business feuds, it's hard to believe that the lessons have to be learned over and over. There are books and books about how to effectively and efficiently pass a business from one generation to the next. I won't rewrite them here; but there is one overriding lesson I can't avoid. There was a time, early on, when our families should have sat down and decided on a plan for allowing any of the shareholders to leave. There should have been a clear valuation method, agreed to by all of the parties, before anyone had any concrete plans to leave. The original consolidation should never have taken place before that agreement was in writing.

It's almost like saying you should consistently back up your computer files, but never doing it until after you've lost everything in a hard-disk crash (sometimes repeatedly); but it is sound advice.

Here's the other lesson that I have learned personally. If you put yourself in a bargaining position in which the other side realizes that you have too big a stake personally, there becomes no way to be bought out. The law clearly says that the majority can't be forced to buy out the minority, and can't be forced to sell out to the minority. Ultimately, the original agreement should include a stipulation that if the majority is not willing to pay the predetermined price for the minority's shares, the minority can buy out the majority, based on the predetermined majority value of the shares. It was a tragic error to determine the value of the buyout so late in the game, when there was clearly no desire by the Fultons to leave our family business.

If there is any other major point I would like to make, it is this. The biggest obstacle to succeeding at anything is the lack of persistence when times get tough. I watched a special on World War II recently on PBS. What amazed me most was how badly things were going in that war for the first couple of years. In today's world, I'm not sure we would have had the guts to continue the fight, no matter how noble the cause. I'm not comparing our challenges in any way to the sacrifice and valor of those times. The point I am making is that, in anything that is worthwhile, even in a business venture, almost all success comes after most of those involved have thrown in the towel. It seems that sometimes, opposition comes from those who should be invested in success.

Finally, I believe the challenge in a family business (or a closely held corporation) is keeping communication open among all of the family members, even those not directly involved in the management of the operations. It is most important that communication be clear as to where each family member sees their involvement in the future of the company. If there are differences, which are openly expressed early, you will be better able to determine how to solve them. At least everyone will know where they stand.

Epilogue

There were so many characters involved in our journey, it's almost impossible to keep up with them. I've always been intrigued by how life is set up in episodes. During each episode, new characters are introduced, some characters remain, and others move on. I would love to find a way to go back and discuss what happened to us with everyone involved, but that's not really the way it works. Over the years, our family has considered "the lawsuit" as a pivotal time in our lives. I'm sure it provides memories for so many who were intimately involved. Thankfully, life has moved on, providing new challenges, momentary failures, and successes.

The Finch Companies survived those times and began growing again after we returned to power. I returned to my position as president and chairman. My brother, Danny, once again became senior vice president. My Dad was finally allowed to enjoy his retirement, which he was in the process of doing when we were thrown out.

Bruce Byrd had been "demoted" by Walt Hayes from vice president of operations to operations manager. When we returned, he was again made vice president. Marcia Washam, who had worked for Finch since she was in high school, was named vice president for quality. Marcia and Bruce were responsible for our achieving the ISO 9005 designation. At the time we earned that designation, there were only two other warehousing operations in the United States who had achieved that honor.

Mom had made the huge sacrifice of letting Sonny have the Furniture Leasing Concepts (FLC) division as a compromise to end the negotiations. When the entire staff of FLC left the new owners and came to Finch, we were happy to hire them for our benefit. Betsy Swinson became our controller, with the remaining office staff working in sales and clerical positions. Three years later, Mom and this staff founded a new furniture leasing business called Interiors Now, which is thriving today. We located this new venture in an office/retail center we built called Fulton Square. Jeff Sims moved from our trucking business to handle operations at Interiors Now. My mother always looked to Jeff as her right-hand man, as we still do today.

In the late 1990s, we had grown the warehousing business to a point in which we occupied more than 1 million square feet of space. Included in that space was a 230,000-square-foot warehouse which we purchased from Delchamps, then a locally owned grocery chain. At the time we purchased it, Scott Paper was occupying clearly 80 percent of our space. They had been our largest customer for more than thirty years. Kimberly-Clark bought them out and assured us that we had a strong future with them. Then the paper industry in Mobile took a major nosedive. Again, I had expanded too fast. We eventually had to downsize and the personnel cuts I had to make were heartbreaking.

Louise Cotton had been with Finch for thirty years and had been treated very shabbily during the time we were removed. Louise is such a trooper, stubborn in the good sense of the word, that as much as the interim administration had tried to get her to quit, she made it her mission to stay on. She was one of the people we had to let go when we downsized. Fortunately, for us, after we got back on our feet, she agreed to come back and is again a vital part of our warehousing division.

One of the toughest moments of my career came when I had to let Bruce Byrd and Marcia Washam go during the downsizing. Bruce went on to become a key player for IPPSCO Steel Company and has been very successful there. Marcia started her own successful office cleaning business. We knew she would be successful because of her dedication to customer service. When the need came for Interiors Now to hire a customer service representative, we asked Marcia to come back with us. We were thrilled when she agreed to come aboard again, and she is still earning respect as a leader in customer service.

It has become a badge of honor to have been hired more than one time by the Finch Companies. Our internal joke is that if you've only been hired one time by Finch, you're still a rookie. Over the years, we've had many people leave Finch only to return for second or third duties. Ed Alexander is a perfect example. Ed got crossways with Walt and was fired, hired the next day by my mother, forced out the next day by Walt and the attorneys, then hired upon our return to eventually run our packaging operation. Ed unfortunately got caught up in our downsizing in the late nineties, but I wouldn't hesitate to bring him on board again if the opportunity came.

Bart Ray was brought on board during our trucking division growth prior to the lawsuit. We thought he had enormous abilities and felt that, if given time and resources, he would be able to grow our fleet to at least 100 tractors. When Hayes and Sonny sold the trucking division, Bart moved on to work for another start-up trucking company. They reached the same goal of more than 100 tractors within a few years.

We will never forget our attorneys. Over the years, members of that firm have told me that our case remains one of their top two or three most memorable cases…I'm not sure that's a good thing. Brock Gordon eventually retired from law and is now living in Big Canoe, Georgia. Alan Christian is still practicing with Johnstone, Adams, Bailey, Gordon, & Harris. Our corporate attorney was Watson Smith, who is now representing a local hospital, but remains close to the Johnstone, Adams, Bailey, Gordon, & Harris firm.

Sonny has retired from Congress after eighteen years in office. He has a consulting practice in the same building that houses Furniture Leasing Concepts, now called FLC Living. His daughter, Shawn Cushing, runs the FLC Living business, assisted by Scott Callahan.

Judge Braxton Kittrell has retired, as has Walt Hayes. Walt had taken over the Furniture Leasing business for Sonny when we returned to Finch. A short time later he left their employ.

We have made some changes in the Finch Companies in the past few years. When my mother died in 2003, I moved out to Interiors Now. Interiors Now is a division of the Finch Companies, of which I am still president and chairman of the board. We decided to become debt-free in our warehouse logistics operations by selling our warehouse buildings to a trucking company. We then partnered with Larry Tomlinson and leased a portion of those buildings to continue our warehouse logistics operations. My brother, Danny, is the leader of Finch Warehouse Logistics and is responsible for all of those operations.

My wife, Lane, has taken over the management duties of Interiors Now. Jeff Sims handles the operations there, with Marcia Washam handling corporate housing and model homes. Lane brings a great deal of experience in the retail area, along with much more taste than I could have ever had.

I still handle many of the corporate level relationships, but with Lane's support I'm pursuing my dream of becoming a professional speaker. When I was younger and active with the Jaycees, I had the opportunity to travel throughout the United States as a motivational speaker. I've always wanted to become a professional speaker, and now my dream is coming true. This book has made it possible for me to travel throughout the country; using the lessons learned from my experience of this travesty, as tools to prevent such unfortunate events from happening to so many others who are involved in family business.

Every human being goes through major challenges throughout his or her life...this is just one. All of those stories, like this one, demonstrate that life isn't neat and smooth. No matter how much we wish it were so, there is no perfect way to live. From my experience in this battle, as well as others, I hope to help people deal with disappointment and temporary failure so that the good times are even sweeter.

As we see so often nowadays, especially in the political arena, it seems that the goal is to tear down those trying to accomplish something rather than to offer supportive ways to succeed. It's the old zero-sum game...if you succeed, I must fail; if you fail, I succeed. That's not useful in politics, and it is certainly destructive in a family business.

What we experienced didn't have to happen. Nor does it have to happen to anyone else. I am dedicating my speaking career to addressing the real-life issues of communication, succession, and preservation of the family business. You can do the hard work now to prevent the heartache later!

Appendix One
July 7, 1988

Dear Tom,

After extensive research into the financial condition and earnings potential of The Finch Companies, Inc., I have determined a price Danny & I are willing to pay for Sonny's 4890 shares in the company. The last three years have been among the most profitable in the history of the company, and we, perhaps optimistically, projected these high returns into the next ten years. The chart below contains some key figures for the last few years.

(000s)	1985	1986	1987	AVERAGE
Total Revenue	$3,925	$4,297	$4,803	$4,342
Total Expenses	$3,701	$4,038	$4,438	$4,059
Net Income	$ 224	$ 259	$ 365	$ 283
% Profit	5.7%	6.0%	7.6%	6.5%
HLC—(48.9%)	$ 110	$ 127	$ 179	$ 138
HLC—Salary	12	12	12	12
Total	$ 122	$ 139	$ 191	$ 150
After Taxes (33%)	$ 82	$ 93	$ 128	$ 101

It is important to realize that beginning in 1988, The Finch Companies, Inc. can no longer afford to pay out 100% of the profits to the stockholders each year. No financial advisor would suggest that 100% of profits be paid out, especially with the plans for expansion that the management envisions. Again, this is the only reasonable direction for an ongoing business concern.

Our bankers have told us that they do not extend consideration of the value of yearly dividends past a ten year period. Assuming a continuing average annual profit of $283,000 for the next ten years, the average after-tax payout + salary to Sonny (if Finch paid 100% in dividends) would be $101,000 per year. Assuming, again optimistically, that those funds could be invested at 10% per year, the present value of that string of payments for the next ten years is $620,605.

With all of this in mind, we are willing to purchase Sonny's stock for $1,000,000 cash, which is equal to $204.50 per share for 4,890 shares, subject to our ability to obtain financing on terms satisfactory to us, and subject to the execution of a purchase agreement satisfactory to both parties and to our respective attorneys. Any amount Sonny owes Finch at the date of purchase would be offset and applied against this amount. This proposal is good until August 1, 1988.

We feel this amount is much more than would be generated in dividends over the next ten years to Sonny. Please understand that this is the top offer, and while we hope and believe it should be accepted, any higher price would simply limit our ability to manage the company's fiscal responsibilities.

Please consider this proposal and let us know of your decision as soon as possible, but no later than August 1, 1988. We look forward to hearing from you.

Yours truly,
Tommy Fulton

Appendix Two
August 1, 1988

Dear Tommy,

I have reviewed yours of July 7, 1988 with Sonny. The purpose of the offer to sell that was made to you was to attempt to find something that was both fair and reasonable to both parties. As you will recall, in order to insure that this could occur, we suggested that prior to any offer being made, agreement be reached by the parties that an offer to sell would constitute an offer to buy. That approach was rejected by you because, as I understand it, you have no desire to sell.

It is, of course, most desirable for these issues to be faced now rather than subsequently handled in a testamentary trust whose trustee has a fiduciary responsibility to maximize the return from the asset without regard to family relationships. We would expect that a trustee would feel that the substantial real estate assets of the company were being underutilized and that, therefore, prudent business judgment properly exercised by management would dictate that either management substantially increase the return from these assets or liquidate them. We would further expect that a trustee, being naturally conservative, would caution against any speculative new business venture undertaken by the company particularly any venture that would result in an immediate adverse effect upon the receipt of dividends.

We believe that the computations of value, upon which the July 7, 1988 offer was based are defective in a number of respects, including, without limitation, the following:

1. The offer is based upon a computation of "Net Income" which simply averages the "Net Income" for the years 1985, 1986 and 1987. When the company's income indicates steady and consistent growth, based upon not only its business, but inflation, it is inappropriate to utilize such an average to establish an artificially low income stream. We believe it is more appropriate to simply consider the 1987 year. This approach is conservative in that neither the company's growth

nor inflation are taken into account in forecasting the future years. An alternative approach would be to utilize a weighted average of the three years and then factor in inflation and reasonable company growth. In either event, a simple average of the three years is unrealistic.

2. In addition, in arriving at "Net Income," the July 7, 1988 offer deducts from total revenues all tax expenses incurred by the company, regardless of whether those expenses are real or simply something artificially provided by the tax code. It is inappropriate to deduct non-cash expenses such as depreciation on buildings from the calculation of the income stream. All such tax deductions which do not cost the company money were factored out of our computation and should be factored out of yours. Accordingly, the "Total Expenses" set forth in the July 7, 1988 offer are overstated.

3. We do not understand the rationale of your attempt at evaluating our client's stock based upon the "After Tax Value" of "Your Share" of the company's "Net Income." It is inappropriate to take into account any assumed tax liability of our client on the "Dividend Potential" of the company. His stock is valued without regard to any such tax liability. For instance, should he die tomorrow, and his entire estate pass to Karen, there may be no tax liability whatsoever.

4. The offer clearly indicates that substantial assets are being underutilized which may be a violation of the reasonable business judgment rule. As you may recall, the Capitalized Income Approach and the Net Asset Approach both yielded a derived value of approximately $3,500,000.00. It is remarkable that the two methods yielded such similar values. The evaluation of an interest must take into account more than the company's dividend paying capacity. If Sonny's prorate share of the net assets of the company are worth $3,500,000.00 but the income stream from those assets yields a stock value of only $1,000,000.00, then it is conclusively established that the assets are being under utilized to the detriment of the stockholders.

5. The July 7, 1988 offer eluded [sic] to the possibility that the company may not, in the future, continue to pay out 100% of its profits to the stockholders. This, of course, would have no effect upon the value of our client's interest since any

undistributed profits should increase the value of the company itself, unless, of course, the undistributed profits were invested in some risky new venture or were used to discharge additional debt on already underutilized assets, both of which may be to the detriment of the stockholders. While the Board might decide to direct employed management to retain earnings, the decision is vested entirely with the Board and must be decided at a properly called Board meeting. As I am sure you are aware, even the Board doesn't have a carte blanche to effect the rights of the stockholders.

It is possible that the basis of the July 7, 1988 offer may simply be that you and Danny feel that you cannot afford to pay more. The purpose of Sonny's offer was to give to the company an opportunity to purchase, over a long period of time at a set price, Sonny's stock without regard to the company's continual improvement in its earnings. It was based on the value of the company and not on either what someone could afford to pay or Sonny could afford to receive.

Sonny feels that his offer was fair and reasonable. He would like to meet with you to discuss his offer and your response. If you can point out to him how you consider his offer to be wrong, he would like to make all appropriate adjustments.

Would you please let me know when a meeting can be arranged.

Best regards,
Victor T. Hudson
For the firm

Appendix Three
August 9, 1988

Dear Tom,

Thank you for your response to our offer to purchase Sonny's stock for $1,000,000. We appreciate all of your effort in these negotiations, but we feel that it is apparent that there will be no agreement in the immediate future on the purchase price for Sonny's stock. With that in mind, we are terminating our offer and will no longer be in need of your services in this regard.

Tom, we felt that we offered our best shot, in good faith, and are disappointed that it was not accepted. However, should Sonny reconsider, we will be most happy to open discussion on this matter with him in the future.

Yours truly,
Tommy Fulton, President
The Finch Companies, Inc.

Appendix Four
September 11, 1989

Dear Tommy:

Sonny, as you may be aware, is suffering from the abrupt discontinuance of payments from The Finch Companies. This has caused him severe financial hardship. He has been caused to invade his retirement account five years early even though it was necessary to pay a penalty of approximately 40% to do so. He is now invading the fund set aside for his children's college education and could, if things continue, lose his home.

Prior to this change in distribution of profits, if the company had $400,000 in profit, approximately $200,000 was distributed to Sonny to be applied to his compensation and for the reduction of his advance account. Under the present plan, only $100,000 is distributed for that purpose and $100,000 kept as retained earnings. Since the company is a Subchapter S corporation, Sonny must pay tax on both the portion distributed and the portion kept as retained earnings. The result is that if the company has $400,000 in profit, $66,000 in tax is due on Sonny's share. Additionally, Sonny is being charged 11% interest on his advance account which is now said to stand at $300,000. Accordingly, when interest and taxes are added together, that consumes $99,000. If only $100,000 is distributed to Sonny and $100,000 kept as retained earnings, the obvious result is that his advance account is reduced by only $1,000 per year so that, at that rate, it would take 300 years to pay out his advance account. Of course, Sonny disagrees that this new method of distribution is appropriate.

The dilemma that has been created underscores the necessity of consummating a buy-out, if at all possible. Sonny is very disappointed that there has been no conversation about an appropriate price.

I was concerned, from the beginning, that a negotiation might lead to hard feelings. For that reason, I first suggested to Charles Chambliss [sic] that you all agree to arbitrate the price with each of you selecting one arbitrator and the two arbitrators selecting the third. When Charles communicated to me that that was unsatisfactory to you,

I then suggested that the best way, in family situations, to assure fairness was to provide that an offer to sell was also an offer to buy, i.e. if Sonny offered to sell his stock to you for $3,500,000.00, you would have the option of either accepting that offer or requiring Sonny to buy your stock from you at an equivalent pro rata price. That approach was also rejected. Now what has occurred is that Sonny made an offer, you made a counteroffer, and the negotiations ended.

Perhaps, rather than debating the value of the company's assets and real estate, the best approach would be to simply make an equitable division of the assets with 49% of those assets being distributed to Sonny. Sonny would be willing to assume the pro rata share of the company's debt on those assets. If you desire, he would enter into leasing agreements with the company so that the company could continue to operate with his share of the assets. It seems to me that this approach is fair to both sides and does not make it necessary to argue about what the values may be. If you feel differently, I would very much appreciate your pointing out to me where I am mistaken.

In any event, I think it is essential for the well being of The Finch Companies and for the well being of your family, that this entire matter be put behind all of you. If my proposal is unacceptable, will you please offer an alternative proposal to avoid further family pain and hardship. I would very much appreciate having an opportunity in the next several weeks to talk with you. I will be glad to accommodate your busy schedule.

Best regards,
Victor T. Hudson

Appendix Five
December 20, 1989

Dear Sonny,

Both of our families have struggled considerably in the last few years with the challenge of determining a fair and equitable way to resolve our differences concerning the ongoing direction of The Finch Companies, Inc. While both sides have made offers and counter-offers, neither of us seemed to be able to agree to each other's valuation of the company. Because you and I could not come to agreement, Mom decided to determine the best way to begin distributing her stock to us as soon as possible, in order to avoid considerable estate problems in the future.

As you know, it is necessary to value the shares of stock at a reasonable market value so that penalties are not assessed to either my parents (in the form of taxes on the amount passed down that is in excess of allowable gifts), or to the estate (in the form of taxes on any undervalued stock). In her effort to make sure that what she gifted to Danny and me was valued properly, Mom asked the firm of Ernst & Young to determine a fair market value of the company.

At this point, I received a letter from Tom Hudson stating that you were still interested in selling your shares, and asking us to make an offer, or show why your original offer should not be accepted. With this in mind, Mom then asked Ernst & Young to determine, in a professional manner, the worth of the company as a whole, as well as the worth of your 48.9% of the company's shares.

It was, and is, in the best interests of all concerned that the stock in Finch be valued realistically, and in a manner that can be justified to the IRS in the future. If valued too high, the company would be subject to taxes far above its worth, and of course, above its ability to pay. This would result in the liquidation of the company. If valued too low, the estate would be subject to fines and additional taxes by the IRS, who are not particularly known to be lenient when called on to do their own valuation.

It is important to know also that, when a price is paid for stock, any estimated valuation, no matter how well defined, automatically becomes the "fair market value." Should Mom begin gifting stock to Danny and me, at the value determined through the analysis of Ernst & Young, for example, any substantially different price paid within three years of the last gifting, changes the value of those gifts, and subjects Mom to tax on the difference.

Ernst & Young assigned people from their Atlanta office who are experienced in this field to prepare a "tentative and preliminary" valuation. I will not attempt to reiterate what they did in determining their results, but will be happy to present their report to you for your scrutiny. Also, since they spent a lot of time researching the company, feel free to ask any questions about any information used by them from anyone here. I hope we can come to agreement on a figure, and feel certain that, while the cash flows will be tight, we have already determined that we can secure the financing to make this work.

Ernst & Young used two main approaches in determining the value of the company stock. The first was the Market Approach, which is a comparison of our company to publicly traded firms which may be similar. The second method was the Income Approach, which indicates the value based on the present worth of future economic benefits. Those approaches yielded the following valuations for the company as a whole:

Market Approach...$2,150,000
Income Approach...$2,000,000

In their analysis, Ernst & Young assigns a discount of 20% to stock value that does not result in majority ownership. This is obviously because investors are infinitely more interested in controlling those rights assigned to the majority, (i.e. electing directors, appointing officers, dividend payments, etc.). Therefore, if the purchase of stock does not result in control of the company, the income approach would value the stock at $1,600,000.

Also, Ernst & Young applies a discount for marketability which represents a reduction in the value of the overall company because it is private and closely-held and, therefore, its stockholders have no access to an active public market in the company's shares. Well documented studies on marketability discounts for closely-held companies have been done and the normal discount is approximately 35%. However, due primarily to the company's history of profitability and other factors, they deemed a 20% discount not unreasonable.

Therefore, the following chart represents their conclusions on the valuation of The Finch Companies, Inc.:

	Total Equity	Per Share*
I. Income Approach	$2,000,000	$200.00
II. Market Approach	$2,150,000	$215.00
III. Conclusion		
100% Value Controlling Interest Basis	$2,000,000	$200.00
Less 20% Marketability Discount	$400,000	$40.00
Less 20% Minority Discount	$320,000	$32.00
100% Value on a Minority Basis	$1,280,000	$128.00
Value of 48.9% Minority Interest (Rounded)	$626,000	$128.00

*10,000 Shares Outstanding

Sonny, I would also like to bring up the offer we previously made, which relies on the amount of income you could reasonably expect to receive from the company for the next ten years, given the unlikely scenario of high profits for each of those years. I believe that you and I agree that 1987 was a very good year for the company, and represents a high level of profitability. In any case, I hope that level of profitability would provide a good base year for the following analysis.

For the sake of this analysis, let's assume that we are able and willing to pay 100% of profits each year to the stockholders as dividends. In 1987, your after-tax dividends amounted to $128,000. If you were to apply a present value factor of 12% to that stream of payments, (assuming, optimistically, that you could invest that money currently in a safe vehicle at that rate), the present value would be roughly $725,000. Keep in mind again, that Finch will realistically need to build up the equity in the company and improve our cash flow status, and therefore will be forced to distribute no more than 50% of profits to the stockholders as dividends.

Even after receiving the analysis from Ernst & Young, and after much research on our part, we are willing to go the extra step and offer you $1,000,000 for your 4,890 shares. We have researched our ability to pay this amount, and believe we can do this in the following manner:

Down Payment in Cash..$150,000

Monthly Payments on note
from us to you for $850,000..................................$12,195

Monthly Payments on note
from you to us for $335,000................................. $ 4,806

Your monthly net would be......................................$ 7,389

Also, since your tax liability will only be due on that amount actually paid, you will be able to offset that, to some extent, by the interest paid on your note to us. At the end of the ten years, you would have been paid $1,613,400. If the dividend to you for 1989 is as much as $50,000, the debt you owe to Finch would be reduced to roughly $285,000, decreasing your payments to us to $4,089 per month, which would increase your monthly net to $8,106.

Tom Hudson asked us to show why his original offer was not valid, and I think the following explanations will do that. [At this point of the letter, I simply reiterated the findings from the Ernst & Young rebuttal to Hudson's valuation, as shown beginning on page 41.]

Sonny, we have done all we can think of to insure that you are offered a fair and reasonable price for your stock. In fact, we have offered more than any advisor has been able to show us that it is worth. Please take time to go over this proposal, and let us know as soon as possible if we can come to agreement. Once Mom starts gifting her shares to us, at the price determined through the valuation, it will be difficult to substantially alter the purchase price.

I would appreciate any questions from you, and hope for a positive answer soon. Thank you for your consideration.

Yours truly,
Tommy Fulton

THE FORUM FOR
FAMILY BUSINESS
ADDRESSING REAL-LIFE ISSUES OF COMMUNICATION
SUCCESSION AND PRESERVATION

Tommy Fulton has worked in his family business since the age of fourteen. Many members of his extended family have also worked there from time to time. When he became the third-generation president, he dealt firsthand with the challenges inherent in succession from one generation to the next. After years in the business, and with all of the experiences described in *An Act of Congress*, he decided to become a professional speaker.

Tommy's first foray into professional speaking was as a motivational speaker, using humor to point out how to address the challenges which face everyone throughout their lives. While he received rave reviews for those speeches, audiences asked again and again about the real-life experiences he and his family endured during the lawsuit. After writing this book, Tommy realized that his experience could help other family business owners, as well as closely held business shareholders. Life teaches lessons, and if we can learn from others rather than endure our own pain... all the better.

Tommy speaks mainly to associations with small business ownership components, addressing the real-life issues of communication, succession, and preservation. His keynote is also invaluable to those who advise businesses, including attorneys, CPAs, financial advisors, and any professional serving the future existence of those businesses. While the topic is very serious, Tommy has the ability to make you laugh and shake your head as you listen to very recognizable indicators of possible trouble.

For more information and to book Tommy for your convention or conference, please contact him via:

The Forum for Family Business
www.ForumForFamilyBusiness.com
www.tommyfulton.com